M000233088

WHAT'S THAT LADY DOING?

WHAT'S THAT LADY DOING?

False starts and happy endings

LOU SANDERS

BLINK

bringing you closer

First published in the UK by Blink Publishing
An imprint of The Zaffre Publishing Group
A Bonnier Books UK company
4th Floor, Victoria House
Bloomsbury Square,
London, WC1B 4DA
England

Owned by Bonnier Books
Sveavägen 56, Stockholm, Sweden

Hardback – 9781788708579
Ebook – 9781788708593
Audio Digital Download – 9781788708609

All rights reserved. No part of the publication may be reproduced, stored in a retrieval system, transmitted or circulated in any form or by any means, electronic, mechanical, photocopying, recording or otherwise, without prior permission in writing of the publisher.

A CIP catalogue of this book is available from the British Library.

Designed by Envy Design Ltd
Printed and bound by Clays Ltd, Elcograf S.p.A.

1 3 5 7 9 10 8 6 4 2

Copyright © Lou Sanders, 2023

Lou Sanders has asserted her moral right to be identified as the author of this Work in accordance with the Copyright, Designs and Patents Act 1988.

Every reasonable effort has been made to trace copyright holders of material reproduced in this book, but if any have been inadvertently overlooked the publishers would be glad to hear from them.

Blink Publishing is an imprint of Bonnier Books UK
www.bonnierbooks.co.uk

This book is dedicated to the only people
who I hope don't read it – my family

Contents

Author's Note

Hello and thank you for buying or stealing a copy of this book. It really means a lot to me.

I sort of feel like I have to give you my credentials at the start, I think that's a thing people do. So, please don't think I'm a bragger. This is just so you know you can trust me. So, I've been barred from an osteopath's for 'crossing the line', I once rugby tackled a security guard for a towel, and I got a 2.2 from one of the bottom universities in England! Treat me as your sage.

Everyone has stories, and these are mine. I didn't think it was possible for me to be happy, but now, a lot of the time, I am. After I've jotted down my burning resentments of the day, of course.

This book is about growing up as a little scamp and slowly sorting myself out. It's about learning from my mistakes, laughing at my mistakes but, crucially, moving on from my mistakes. Leaving behind only the shame (and the stories).

I hope you enjoy it. x

He is a spicy character, and while spices are popular, they can stain things forever.

How Do
You Play?

I grew up around Ramsgate and Broadstairs in the eighties and nineties. They were relatively safe seaside towns right next to each other in Thanet. Pretty, quiet and at the end of the line. Margate was, and still is, their more famous, naughtier sister. Ramsgate had a big harbour and used to be a bit rougher than Broadstairs, but it did boast a Tammy Girl, a Peacocks, *and* a New Look – so fashion-wise, it was not fucking about. Broadstairs was a bit more middle class, you know, an-old fashioned sweet shop, a haberdashery, and three off licences.

These three small neighbouring towns are a little frayed around the edges, but they have a laid-back, blue-skied charm. I love the faded glamour of an old seaside town:

the pastel colours of an ice cream parlour, the peeling paint in an old theatre, a ceremonial band-stand, some territorial seagulls and a holiday spirit hanging in the air.

I loved Thanet, with its cabbage patches and its corn fields, but I yearned for more. I used to wear blue glittery trousers with massive orange platform boots, and then say things like 'What are they looking at? Geez this town is so small-minded.' And once you've been that much of a bellend, you really do need to leave.

My theory is people are less ambitious by the sea – they walk slower, they talk slower, they drink more, life is less of a race and more of a picnic. That could be a compliment or an insult, depending on how you view capitalism.

In some ways, it was a relatively simple time, but human beings always find a way to make things complicated. When I was little, I would ask my brother how to 'play', as if there were rules and I could get it wrong. I'd just be looking at these plastic figures thinking, What now? I don't know, make them walk? Make them talk to each other? But what about?

I did feel like I got a lot of stuff wrong, that I was somehow wrong. I imagine a lot of people feel like that. I remember once, when I was about ten, I was using the house phone and my mum said, 'Why are you dialling on the phone like that? Try to add some style to it, your dad had style; he did things with a bit of flair.'

HOW DO YOU PLAY?

I'm sure she was trying to help but her frustration let me know that even my mum thought I was a bit of a loser. For clarification, I was just using a phone in the standard way, I wasn't headbutting it or anything.

Before we go any further, there's a lot of stuff I won't be saying about my family because most of them are still alive lol. If any of them drop before the paperback comes out, I'll whack it in then.

None of my family want me to talk about them in my book, but for some reason I feel compelled to. Sorry, everyone. But I will try to be fair and I am leaving out anything which means I will be disinherited – so yes, I guess I am a good person. To be honest, I don't think there's a lot to inherit, so there's another reason why I have to write this book. Plus, the person who comes out the worst in these stories is me (takes a bow).

I am grateful for my parents; they did their utmost with what they had at the time. I am grateful for every single thing that life has given and taken, because it's allowed me to grow. Without feeling invisible, I wouldn't have done comedy. Without feeling lost, I wouldn't have found spiritual answers. And without pissing myself in a Ryman's, I wouldn't have given up alcohol. The Lord works in mysterious ways (and stationers).

I would tell you now how much I loved my older brother and how much I looked up to him and how funny and kind he was, but he has assured me that if

3

I mention him personally, he will 'suit up and take me to court'. So after this page I will barely mention him. Basically, *you* have to lose him so that I don't have to! So just one last word on him because he really did help inform my personality (and that's the sentence he's going to hate the most).

When we were little and living in Ramsgate, life was fun. It was after my dad had been sent packing when I was two, and before my stepdad was on the scene when I was four. It was just our little trio: my brother, my mum and I. A well-balanced triangle. Sometimes my mum would take us potato picking for money, we loved running around a big field. The house was full of mums and kids, we had friends at the end of the garden and every day after school we'd get a '10p mix-up, no bubble gum'.

Once my brother and I decided our duvets looked like snail shells, so we wrapped them around us, snuck out of the house and started crawling up the pavement with our homes on our back, making snail noises. You know the noise a snail makes? No, neither did we. But when you're crawling up the road with a duvet on your back, it's important to commit to the role.

Our neighbour Ernie delivered us back to our mum. Ernie was cool AF. He gave me and my brother a toy tool set once and my bro nearly exploded with excitement. Ernie was like a father figure. He was a salt-of-the-earth mechanic, and was married with a grown-up son. He had big hands, a big heart and a big chuckle – we loved him. Come to think of it, it wasn't like we saw him a lot, we probably only saw him ten times in our lives, but he had a big impact. I wonder if he ever knew.

A short time after this, my mum met my stepdad, and our life upgraded financially (he was a teacher, and she only worked here and there around school runs), and so, at some point they bought a bigger house together. We didn't care about house size. But we had two front rooms! One for us and one for my stepdad. My mum thought that might help.

My mum and stepdad met at a folk club and my mum fancied his friend but he was taken. When I asked my stepdad about it, he said he really fancied her, and it was love at third sight.

My stepdad's favourite colour was brown and he used to be a train spotter. Sounds pretty dull, doesn't it? And yet, he made life hell until I moved out at fifteen. He hated noisy children and we were noisy children. The older we got, the meaner he was. My mum was in the middle like a rabbit in the headlights. This is obviously just my side of the story, but good luck getting his, because he's dead. I didn't do it!

My real dad and stepdad could not have been more different. When my mum met my dad he was a bit of a Jack-the-lad; sold encyclopaedias, then hearing aids, had a taxi rank, then a fish and chip shop. The businesses would often fail and he'd get up and start again. Remarkable really. A very upbeat man. Sticky-out ears, headset, flat cap, we don't have a lot in common, but you'd like him. About fifteen years ago he used to have a burger van off a motorway in Milton Keynes – he'd sell burgers, sure, but he'd also sell plastic belts and power drills, and some under-the-counter porn videos – make your hobby your job, guys! It was a different time (you probably got that from the mention of 'videos').

My mum and real dad got married after about six months of dating. I asked her how he had wooed her and she said he took her for dinner?! When they got married my mum was in a brown dress and hat and Dad was in a big purple suit with flares. He looks like a big character, well, short, but with big-flare energy. My mum's parents didn't come to the wedding because they didn't approve of him. After she kicked him out and the marriage was annulled (bigamy), I think my mum then thought, Right, I'll go for the opposite man, someone very safe. I can see how she arrived at that: my stepdad wore glasses, talked about ISAs and was severely risk-averse.

When my mum was younger, before I burst out of her butthole, she had a motorbike and smoked doobies and was a bit of an outlier. She is a very bright, interesting woman and I think she could have been a great artist, but she had to leave art college when her dad got ill. She didn't do art for most of her life because there were 'lots of people better than me'.

To give you an idea about her confidence holding her back, she once did the most magical kids' book, which she illustrated beautifully. She sent it off to one publisher. They replied that they didn't publish children's books. And that's it, she never sent it to anyone again. Dejected from just one answer from a place that didn't do kids' books. That's like me feeling let down that Clarks Shoes won't buy my comedy special. And I am!!

My mum is two different people: one so compassionate, artistic, positive and spunky; and one an injured bird pecking away at itself. She's the type of person who can be quite manipulative, but she's such a sweetheart that she tells you to 'watch out because I can be quite manipulative… and I'm only going to get worse'! You've got to love that warning.

I would always try to minimise my mum's stress. I was a real Goody Two-shoes at primary and junior school, because I wanted my mum to be relaxed. If anyone else in the family upset her I would take it quite personally.

When mum was fun, she was super-fun. Even recently at seventy-four she was jumping over the neighbours' fence and doing some guerrilla gardening, cutting down their shrubs that had grown amok while they were away. She could have used the front door, she had a key. I guess that's not as adventurous.

And she's FUNNY. When there's a light in her eyes, she's unrivalled. Once she happened to be dressed all in beige and she found a beige swimming cap with a teat on the end and so she bounced down the stairs singing a song about being a condom: 'I'm a little condom here's my peak, I'm a little condom nice to meet [you]!'

Another time she tried my skates on – downhill – and smacked into a wall, laughing hysterically.

She has the capacity for such humour and warmth, and that's the real her. But when she is anxious, there's no getting through to her, and she causes a flurry of drama. More than once she's decided on Christmas Day that she's not attending the meal, and turned back home to go and be by herself.

I know my mum loved me, but I did subconsciously feel that I was loved the most when I was useful and only now am I realising I've carried that into my adult life with relationships and friendships. I'm forever trying to fix people and make them happy, which is terrible for them and even worse for me. If I fix anything, it's got to be that! I've got to fix the fixer.

In many ways we were very lucky, we got taken to Butlin's holiday camp one year and another time my stepdad did a house swap for a week and we went to Berlin. I'll just let you sit with those two whoppers for a bit! Berlin and Butlin's, baby.

When I was five, I had a party at the house and Mum

made up all her own party games. 'Don't fall into the cow pat' was an absolute thrill, and one of my classiest friends Sadie still talks about it now. We had to dance around some fake cow pats to music and not fall on them. Inspired. And she made us birthday cakes when we were little. That's love. I wouldn't do that. Actually, with my baking skills, it's more loving not to do it. You can just buy them!

She must have taught me how to ride a bike, and how to swim, and I've taken it all for granted. I'm cycling around and swimming up and down, with not even a nod to the old bird. I'd forgotten about when she used to take me to ballet after school. Before the teacher said I was not best suited to ballet (I used to hide at the back because my brother had said my bottom was so huge it was abnormal, so I didn't want anyone to see it).

To be fair, I was never going to be a ballerina. I guess the teacher was putting me out of my misery and she framed it well: 'We think Louise would be better suited to drama.' Damn straight I would, bitch. I love drama!

So it was nice of my mum to try and buy me some grace. I mean, sure, she did tell me that 'all the other mums think we're bad and the other mums are prettier and their daughters are daintier', but that was her insecurity and she was confiding in me because, although I was only ten, I had the butt of a much older woman.

We always think parents should be perfect, but they

have to do everything we have to do, for more people, on less sleep. Judging people is easy – you have an *imaginary* version of what you would have done, but with none of the *non*-imaginary problems they had at the time.

◆ ◆ ◆

My real dad and I didn't see each other much when I was little and we had an awkward relationship until I was a lot older. I think in part because I was always bringing up stuff he'd done, like a weird little sin supervisor. Hands on hips, crime calculator in hand – he must have dreaded my visits. He wanted to move on and let the past be in the past – which is the best ethos.

If you have a compass set to fun, a drive in life and a penchant for framing things in a positive way, I honestly think it's hard to fail. And that's what he had and that's what he gave us. Both biologically and in person. He's very charming, upbeat and fun. He's cheeky. He wears stupid T-shirts that say things like 'save water, drink beer' and has gnomes in the garden who are holding their members. He's often looking for the amusement in life, which is one of the best qualities you can have. He also used to lend me money when I started in comedy and couldn't pay my rent, gawd love him (the second best quality you can have is to lend me money).

He is a spicy character, and while spices are popular,

they can stain things forever. My mum says there were a few times when we were younger when he pretended to be dead in the hope that she'd stop contacting him and making him see us, you know, because he was dead. It's a hell of an excuse. Can you take the kids this weekend? Oh God no, I'm dead!

When we were little, we would spend a week with him once a year and he would look for the F.U.N. He would buy fun. We're talking fairgrounds, the Radio 1 Roadshow, chips for lunch and dinner if we wanted! It was exciting to see a totally different way of life. He took us to theme parks and bought us the latest trainers. He gravitated towards my brother, which my brother needed so I was pleased about that. I did love him but we found it harder to connect. I was absolutely 'team mum'.

Because I technically had two dads who were very different but neither of whom seemed enthralled with me, I was always quite desperate for attention. When I was about six, I came up with a plan to wear a ponytail not at the side, not at the back, but right slap bang in the middle of my face. HANGING IN THE MIDDLE OF MY FACE. I honestly thought, Why has this not been done before? I'm a genius. My mum let me wear it to school. She was good like that, for better or worse, she often encouraged free thinking. So off I went looking absolutely unhinged. Feeling fantastic! My only slight reservation that day was that everyone would copy me. Weirdly, not a lot of takers for the pony in the middle of the face. And when I say not a lot, I mean no one. Obviously. I only wore the fad till the end of the day. I must have picked up from people's faces that it wasn't quite the thing. Did somebody say 'emotionally intelligent'?

Just after this, I was staying at my dad's house and he realised he was going to have to brush my hair after a bath. I can only assume he had never brushed anyone's hair before. He sat me in the middle of the room on a chair, and he brushed a strand of hair about two centimetres wide. He said, 'Hold that' and then brushed another tiny strand: 'Hold that.' I added it to the first strand of hair, and on we went, 'hold that' around the head for what seemed like an hour.

I thought, This is bonkers, I don't think he's quite got the idea here. My mum had never done it like this in her life. But I was so pleased to have the attention, I sat nice and still in case the moment evaporated somehow. I gripped on tight to the fistful of hair and tried not to burst with all the feelings from the inside. My dad was brushing my hair! He loved me and he was brushing my hair! The best ever Christmas gift.

He wouldn't always remember birthdays and Christmases, which I get now. Life is busy, time is an illusion. Kids get too stuck on that shit; I guess it's because they're not as busy and time goes slowly for kids. And quite frankly they've got a lot less in the calendar.

But one year we were seeing him before Christmas, so he gave me my Christmas present early so I could open it in front of him. I could not believe my little mincy spies. It was a huge fairy castle, it seemed so big and luxurious. I was gobsmacked. First the hair – now this present – my gosh – this guy is obsessed with me! Then I found out he got the exact same one for the girl next door; he'd only just moved there, he hardly knew her. Maybe he knew her mum, if you catch my drift. That was genuinely my next thought, as a seven-year-old. Very cynical sleuthing for a seven-year-old. Hopefully it was just 'two for one'. (On the toys, not the local mums.)

As you get older, there's a freedom in accepting and celebrating people as they are, rather than trying to force them into a role they were never made for.

**I am (famously)
a big fan of
the dads.**

How to Make Someone Notice You

Away from the high glamour of fairy castles, in daily life, I was in love with Craig Prentice. A boy at my school who I was obsessed with from the ages of six to ten – my very first addiction. I was obsessed with boys who didn't like me from a very young age. Daddy issues? Yes, yes, I had a subscription!

My first attempt at wooing him was on Valentine's Day. At the weekend I had bought a box of Maltesers for a pound and I secretly took them to school. We kept our school bags hanging on pegs outside of the classroom and I knew which one was Craig's, and with my heart racing, I just slipped the box of choccies into his bag. I don't know what I was hoping for because I don't think I left a note. Maybe I thought he might be so moved, he would hunt down the thoughtful gifter – glass slipper style.

Instead of that, some little turncoat called Kerry with bad eyesight and an actual pony snitched on me. Mr Salmon (yeah, cool name bro) confronted me in front of the whole class. It was so humiliating. To have a crush at that age was the most embarrassing thing in the world. To have it barked out in front of every single classmate, well, that was excruciating.

Still, it didn't put me off trying to make Craig my boyfriend. It wasn't that I was overconfident, I was just demented.

I thought the issue was that Craig hadn't noticed me. I went to a small school and everyone knew each other, so he'd definitely noticed me, but logic doesn't work on seven-year-old me (or current-year-old me) – so for my next trick…

During our PE class, everyone wore black shorts and a white T-shirt. It wasn't even enforced because everyone just wanted to fit in – until 'COOOEY – Loulie might be switching things up a bit here.' So I turned up to PE in a shiny emerald green leotard and leggings. With matching sweatbands. Never stop shining! Mr Motivator was big at the time and I thought I had a foolproof plan. I went to get changed in the toilets to make an entrance. Well, I did that alright. Everyone just stopped and looked at me, and not in a good way. The silence was pierced only by my teacher, Mr fucking Salmon again, scoffing at me and barking that my outfit was, 'A little OTT to say the least.' I didn't know what OTT meant but I could tell it wasn't the celebration I'd hoped for.

If I was a teacher and a kid in my class turned up in that, I don't think I'd be cross like he was. I like to think I would be celebrating their individuality, while trying to hide the fact I was choking with laughter.

Anyway, I was expecting people to ask where I got my shiny outfit, not what I was playing at, and I was so sure of my strategy that I hadn't bought a back-up outfit, so I had to go ahead and play rounders looking and feeling like an absolute prize prune. I was really trying to fade into the background, which is of course very tricky in a skin-tight circus outfit.

Well, Craig noticed me, but it was a no from him.

I would feel sorry for that little girl embarrassing herself in PE, except I don't know how much this dressing-down put a chink her armour. Because only a few months later, she was back at it.

At my primary school, like most others in the land, once a year there are end-of-term photos. And everyone wears a school uniform for the pictures. A letter is even sent home the week before to remind parents to ensure they have the correct uniform and to please make sure 'your child's hair is clean and brushed'. They should have included a diagram for the dads! Just kidding ladz, I am (famously) a big fan of the dads.

So everyone is in their formal, matching school uniform, including me. The queue is snaking towards the photographer. So I seize my moment, go behind a curtain and take off my skirt and shirt, to reveal the same cursed shiny turquoise *Flashdance* ensemble. But this time, judging by the photo I have, I was pretty proud of myself.

So odd that Craig Prentice wasn't into a young Rosemary Conley.

Aim low and you might just hit something!

Barbie and Bestiality

(A Misleading Title)

I love that my mum let me do what I wanted. Perhaps she was following my lead; I was weird anyhow, so maybe she was just letting me express myself. I mean, who wants to wear a uniform every day anyway? Eccentricity is good, it's more interesting, it's exciting. I think on the whole it's positive. Unless of course you are so eccentric, it tips over into bestiality or something. 'That guy's wacky! He sucked off a dog' etc., etc.

My mum really encouraged free thinking. She was vocal about the injustices that we should pay attention to. She told us the history books at school were biased and pointed out examples of racist reporting on the news, which, to be fair, there was a lot of.

Gender was a big topic. Once my mum's friend came to visit and she gave my brother an Action Man. When you threw him out of a window (the Action Man, not my brother), he descended in the most glorious way, parachute floating open, gliding down... what a thrill. We would run upstairs and launch him out of the window, imagining being him and gawping in awe.

This nice lady gave me a baby doll who did nothing. Not to be ungrateful, but I'm very glad my mum explained that I should rip that doll's head off and shit down its neck. She explained that boys' toys tended to be more active and inspirational, whereas girls' toys were more passive, often encouraging us to take a nurturing role. Often little girls are taught they are not the main event and their purpose is to prioritise others. To facilitate the main event.

Mum would point stuff like that out, ahead of her time really; she taught us to be aware of these conditionings and to try and rise above them. Like when a friend of ours got a toy kitchen for her daughter and my mum privately scoffed. I loved being in on this dissection of life, me and Mum.

She believed there should be equality and social mobility in every area, though with us, there was a feeling that our lot was our lot. Our gran didn't think you should show off or want too much, in case someone got the wrong idea. So with that, Mum managed our expectations

22

of what was possible for our lives, reminding us, 'It's not people like us who get fancy jobs,' 'You can't work in TV,' 'Rich men go for a different type of women… it's not people like us.' She wasn't being unkind, she was just trying to save us from getting hurt. Aim low and you might just hit something!

I find family dynamics fascinating; the often invisible patterns that control, mould and shape us. Everything starts with childhood and leads back to it.

Family dynamics are at the heart of everything in our life, long after we've left the nest. Like the limiting beliefs from my gran, passed to my mum, to lil old me, it takes a long time to recognise the damaging patterns and dynamics we are in and then you have to try and overcome them.

Blueprints are hard to transcend because family have the biggest hold on us – perhaps because they are the first to get a hold of us.

I don't think there's a sane family on this planet – there's always something going on. I have read that apparently as little souls we chose our parents for the lessons we need – so if that's true, well done to all three of my parents – you made it! Must have been a helluva lotta competition!

You can outsource the laundry, the decorating, even the gardening, but not your own power.

Popular Isn't Always Better

A ged five, my first best friend was a girl called Sam – she was the most popular girl in the school because she had blonde hair and packed lunches.

The thing is, Sam was quite boring. Once she came round for a playdate and I got excited; I was shouting and swinging off things, rolling around like a one-kid party. My mum said, 'Louise, you need to calm down or Sam will want to go home.' I thought, Erm this chick does not understand kids, what's she on about?

Ten minutes later, Sam was crying and saying she wanted to go home. So I cut loose of that bore and started to hang out with a new girl called Clare. She was trouble and had hot dinners.

I then made best friends with a girl called Vicky Babins and she was sort of perfect. She looked like a cute little chipmunk and was really fun but in a less manic way than Clare and I.

I still loved Craig Prentice and Vicky and I had seen a film where the girl and boy kiss at a party, so we thought, yeah, we just need to have a party. Simple. I have a party and Craig realises that it was the institution of school holding us back. The uniforms, the drudgery, the systematic timekeeping. Once he saw me in the wild, he would realise he loved me. Once he was looking at me over a table of crisps and squash, his heart would kick in.

The only thing was, it wasn't my birthday, so I had to convince my mum to let me have a party in my bedroom. I said I would take care of everything – budget, invite, agenda. I was ten. She said yes. Baffling old business. We were not indulged in any other ways; biscuits were counted and if we needed shoes, they were often a birthday present. So it's mad she just went along with these crazy old whims. But there we are, I was allowed to throw my own party in my bedroom.

I hand drew the invites for the lucky five. They all said yes. Bingo.

Come the day, Vicky and I had a budget of fifty pence. We got five packets of Tangy Toms crisps and laid out some tap water. I had a boom box with a free

Weetabix cassette, paused and ready to rock. Back in the day, if you ate enough Weetabix, you could send off the coupons from the boxes in exchange for a tape of pop hits. Truly, a golden time.

The cassette tape was paused over the only good song on it. Nik Kershaw's 'Wouldn't it be Good'. Ready for Craig's entrance. We'd also stolen one party popper from my mum's bureau ready to pull when the 'main event' walked in. A lot of pressure on this nine-year-old lad.

What I remember from the day is this.

The front door would go, and some children would arrive one by one with their parents. As agreed, my mum just let me deal with things, sometimes poking her head out to say hi as she floated past.

When one mum and kid came in, I remember I said that the party was upstairs in my bedroom, follow me. Already quite weird. The mum came too, perhaps because she was nosy, but more likely thinking, Well, I better just check that this is safe. I'm dropping my kid off in another kid's bedroom. Anyway, fine, I could deal with this, it's not like there was anything bad in the room. There was, in fact, nothing in the room. Then the mum said to their child, while we were on the landing, give Louise her present then. Oh no. Present? They must think it's my birthday. I didn't know what to say.

Rude not to open it, I guess. So I opened the present outside the bedroom door. It was a toy from Woolworths.

I think it was a fancy pen with lots of different colours and a notebook and rubber set. I looked down at it, hot shame on my face. It wasn't my birthday. I didn't deserve presents – this isn't a proper party. It's a pulling party for two people and the other kids are just background artists.

Something in me felt wrong as I opened the door to the party room. No music, some tap water and if you were lucky, a tomato-flavoured crisp.

This kid's mum was visibly perturbed. If she was upset, what would Craig's mum think? Sorry, I should have explained: the party will have some candy. Yeah – some eye candy, it's Craig. The party will have some meat. Yep, it's Craig again, he's the meat, etc.

The party was super lame. Craig came in, we pulled the party popper, it took three attempts. No one really knew what to do. And Craig didn't talk to me, at all. He actually asked Vicky out. Who said yes. Fair enough, I would have, too. Well played, Vicky. I was resigned to this fate. I wasn't even jealous, I think I just thought, Ah yes, that makes sense, I can see why he would like her.

The day after the 'party' we were all queuing up to get our exercise books back, Craig was in front of me and he turned round and made a scornful, mocking face at me. The sort of face that is now unacceptable, unless you are Donald Trump. It's the placing of the tongue in the chin skin, if you get me. Not his fault, he was a nice kid, it was just of its time. I'm sure I did it as well. In fact, I definitely did, we all did. But I don't think we knew why.

Anyhow, when he made a face at me I was a bit confused, but I had just about enough self-awareness to think, Yep, I do think that's about the 'party'.

I've been scared of throwing parties ever since. Years later, I spoke to Craig, as a TV company were going to get him on a show to talk about me stalking him (in a fun, pre-watershed kind of way), but he couldn't make the record. However we got chatting on Instagram, and don't worry, I didn't fancy him. Which was a relief for him, me, and I dare say his wife and kids. He seemed like a very decent family guy.

However, in that brief internet chat he said HE. DID. NOT. REMEMBER. ME. I was in his classes for about six or seven years, at two different schools, and he did not remember me. Maybe given my behaviour that's a good thing. Maybe he was traumatised, so blanked me out. I'm his Vietnam.

He did remember Vicky though. Of course that's how it works, you remember the ones you are thinking about, but not the ones who are thinking about you. CP (Craig to you) said that Vicky stood him up in the park one day, and broke his heart. He also said he thought she had died! I hope she didn't die. I remember her beautiful little pixie face and creamy skin. She was such a cutie, even when for some reason, she had her hair all chopped off. Only very pretty girls can carry off a crew cut. Or even better, ones who don't care! She had a mum that worked a lot and a brother who was a bully and she had big round eyes and a funny laugh.

Craig was much more of a big deal to me because I thought about him all the time, he was etched in forever, like the lyrics to your teenage soundtrack. Whereas I was more of a small nuisance to him, something to be avoided, a pest, a little fly buzzing around.

So often we invest our power in other people, often without them asking us to.

I like getting older, because the older I get, the less I allow people to have power over me – I'm careful not to hand my energy over to someone else.

You can outsource the laundry, the decorating, even the gardening, but not your own power or potential.

But the thing is never about the thing, is it? Sometimes a Claire's Accessories stud is a totem of so much more.

Pontins, Vodka and Belly Rings

When I was about ten, me and my brother went to Pontins with my dad and his girlfriend at the time, Tracey. Tracey had a big perm and used to spritz and scrunch her hair a lot. She wore white stilettos with tall, thin pointy heels that clicked when she walked. I think she liked the impact she could make just by walking; clip clop, clip clop, clip clop, people would have to pay attention to her. Her jeans were so tight we could not fathom how she'd got them on. They were light denim and one pair had denim bows all up the back. I had never seen anything like it. Nor had Pontins Prestatyn.

Tracey wouldn't let our dad touch or hug us because

she got jealous and 'didn't really see the point of children'. Ironically, this was a woman who had over two hundred teddy bears, several Disney jumpers and the glasses of an absolute nonce.

She was probably the same age I am now. Imagine treating two little (and I'm going to say ADORABLE) kids like they were vermin in the gorgeous setting of Wales's second-best Pontins. Impossible if you ask me.

It must have been quite stressful for my dad trying to balance these two worlds. But then it was only once a year.

◆ ◆ ◆

I had my first taste of alcohol at Vicky's house when we were eleven. Her mum was out and it was back in the day when eleven-year-olds let themselves in. I remember being so impressed and envious that Vicky had a whole drawer with crisps and chocolate and biscuits in it and could just have what she wanted. Imagine that for an eleven-year-old – 'Take what you want, kids'. I could not get my nut around it.

I remember telling my mum, and heavily hinting at what a fantastic idea that was. Food would send me loco, I couldn't get enough of it. I remember thinking if I was allowed it all the time, maybe I'd be chill around it like Vicky was. Or maybe I'd be a twenty-stone child, who knows? We were rationed to two biscuits a day and if we took more we got in deep trouble. I don't think they counted the biscuits, who has got the time? But every now and again we were cross-examined.

Anyway, the point is Vicky's mum was relaxed and we thought we would repay her by trying her alcohol. We went for whisky, and I remember the sensation. It was hot and heavy. It was as disgusting as it was thrilling. But it warmed my throat as it went down and then warmed my whole body. It was exciting. It felt like it was a portal to another world. I remember thinking, OK, I'll be back for you.

Even though it was a thrill, I don't remember sipping alcohol again until the age of thirteen when I really bloody went for it. I went to my first nightclub at thirteen, I mean that is absolutely insane that they let me in. I was with some older kids but they were only fifteen. It was a nightclub on Margate seafront, full of underage kids.

In the club, there were some posters of a beautiful fifteen-year-old called Tiffany that the bouncers were not allowed to let in. She had previously been drinking there and her mum found out. Her mum then insisted they put posters up of Tiffany's face to say she was barred because of her age. At that age I think that's one of the most mortifying things that could happen. I'm not saying we would have preferred to be abducted but…

Last I heard Tiffany was modelling in Norway – maybe a talent scout saw the poster!

Anyway, I was in the club, dressed up. I was wearing big, flared crochet culottes with black tights underneath. I sported a hat to age me up a bit, eighteen-year-olds love hats!

Alcohol really excited me, people say it is a depressant but if those people had seen me exploding on the dance floor to Right Said Fred's 'I'm too Sexy' they would have said it was only a depressant for the people watching me. I was having the time of my life, I was thinking this is mad, I'm thirteen – I can't wait to show off at school about this.

When I did show off at school, the kids gave me a reply straight from their parents' gobs: 'If you go clubbing now, what are you going to do at eighteen?' 'Erm, go up to London!'

When I went out past my curfew, I told my mum I was sleeping at my friend Gina's house. Gina's mum let us get away with more because Gina was older, and because her mum had a lot of her own stuff going on – that's my polite spin on it. So, I either stayed at Gina's, or I told my mum I was staying there and then snuck in at 2 a.m. and slept in the porch. I used to hide a sleeping bag in a drawer before I went out. When I wanted to do something, I was quite driven.

So at the age of thirteen it would be fair to say I had a pretty full life. As well as tearing up the dancefloors of the clubs, I was a hard-working, fully employed young woman. I had four jobs. I got up at 6 a.m. Monday to Friday and cleaned the cages at a pet shop. The manager was really annoying, he only paid me £5 a week, and when he sacked me he didn't tell me; he phoned my stepdad and told him instead, with no reason. I thought that was cowardly. I got the job myself by just going in and asking, he'd never met my stepdad.

I mean sure, I may have forgotten to put the rabbit back in the cage and they had a dog, but just tell me that to my face. Anyway, the rabbit was fine and pet shops are ultimately cruel. Especially if I'm working there!

I also had a job washing dishes in a hotel when they needed me, a job at a newsagent's unpacking boxes and cleaning, and then a Saturday job at a different sweet shop. They were on rotation, so it wasn't too bad. It was weekend work and a couple of nights a week and then the pet shop in the mornings. I had a lot of energy and I loved earning money.

My parents would always pay for school trips and books I needed and school uniform (if it wasn't the fancy shoes), but as a kid I had to buy my own deodorant, most of my clothes and my tampons.[1] I've no idea why. I'm sure if I had sat my mum down and said, 'Come on, Mags, pull your finger out and get us some tammies,' she would have, but she couldn't have really wanted to. Still,

---

1   Obviously, I'm more of a Mooncup / period pants girl now. If you are still using throwaway items, do wake up and smell the demise of the planet.

it contributed to me being independent, which is the biggest gift of all.

I went vegetarian at thirteen too, perhaps influenced by the pet shop. My mum was working and a mother of three and didn't have the capacity to make a separate dinner, so she said I would have to make my own, which again forced me to be self-reliant. She also presumed it was just a fad and another bid for attention. I do a lot of things for attention but eating facon isn't one of them.

◆ ◆ ◆

Despite being busy with my social life and many forms of employment, I did find the time to kick back and relax on holiday with the folks. That summer, I was on a camping holiday in France. Just me, Mum, my stepdad and my little half-brother. I had a lot of freedom – I had my own little tent completely to myself – which was nice, and which I abused. One night after dinner, I went off to the trampoline area and I got speaking to these blond brothers who were twins. I think they were fifteen or sixteen years old, so of course I told them I was fifteen. I fancied them both – well, they were identical twins. I slightly preferred the one that could tell the time, as you would do. One genuinely could not tell the time. He just hadn't learnt and now was trying his best to get on board with the whole concept of time.

Anyhow, after a nice bounce and a chat, they both

walked me back to my tent and I was so excited about my new twin friends. But my mum was waiting for me, and when she saw the older, bigger guys dropping me off at night, she shouted at them: 'SHE'S THIRTEEN, SHE'S ONLY THIRTEEN.'

One may have struggled with minutes and hours but they both knew a year when they heard one. They looked horrified, and one of them looked quite hurt and said, 'You said you were fifteen.' They ran away and I never saw them again. Mortifying. I really wanted to kiss them – not both of them, whichever one wanted to the most. Hopefully the one that could read a clock. What time is it? Kissing o'clock.

I felt so bad and so embarrassed for the rest of the holiday and Mum was in a stinking mood with me. Shame all round really. I was so miffed my mum had done that, but looking back, it would be sillier if she hadn't – poor Mumma. I was a bit of a wily one.

Around this time, I got my belly button pierced and when my mum saw it, she slapped me round the face and called me a tart. It must have been a shock and it did look a bit jarring on a kid. But the thing is never about the thing, is it? Sometimes a Claire's Accessories stud is a totem of so much more. She was worried my loose-natured freedom would end up getting me in trouble. And she was absolutely right. It was hard for my mum because I was so headstrong and wild, mixed with incredibly low self-esteem and a penchant for excitement. Some of it was a reaction to a tricky home life, but even without that I might have been bursting away from the seams, desperate to create my own misguided path.

Case in point, and ring in belly, I tried to lose my virginity at thirteen – luckily, we couldn't stuff it in. I don't wish to be radical, but I do think thirteen is a bit on the young side. What's the rush? You can have loads of awful, unfulfilling sex for the rest of your life! In my defence there wasn't a lot of entertainment back then.

My boyfriend at the time was called Kai. He was sixteen and a builder. He had a black puffer jacket, smoked and always smelt heavily of aftershave, a gorgeous novelty. He was thick as shit but did the job. The job being cuddling and snogging. And probably some hand stuff. I loved him. Well, not proper love, but it felt like it. Once I told him he wasn't being romantic enough and the next day he hid about thirty giant packs of Parma Violets (my favourite sweets, would have been weird if I didn't like them) around the little porch of my family's house. I was dancing around on cloud nine. Very Emily Brontë. My very own *Wuthering Heights*.

Kai had his own battles. I think he was adopted and a bit of an outsider in his family and couldn't really articulate himself. I think underneath it all perhaps he was deeper and more emotional than his circumstances and surroundings let him be. But also he was quite dumb. And that's coming from someone who once got a score of eighty in an IQ test. Eighty means a bit of brain damage I think. To be fair to me, I did make a sandwich and take a phone call during the test, because I didn't realise it was timed.

Kai and I tried to have sex twice, once in a bathroom and once in my bedroom, but my body was saying no. Neither of us knew what we were doing and we just tried to stuff it in. We were really confused as to why it wasn't just happening for us. But I seem to remember it was like trying to get soup into a slot machine, so I wouldn't be surprised if he'd been flaccid; it was the first dingle I'd seen.

The body is very clever, it tries to eliminate the things that are bad for it! I'm sorry to my bod for all that I've put her through. We have really been on a journey together and I am eternally grateful for the old girl's strength. It's worth saying that the belly ring forced its way out of my body, too, and I've not put one back in since. And as for dingles – well, that's another story.

Kai must have made bad life decisions, too, because he finished with me! He did quite well with girls. I knew this because we still all knocked about as friends after, so I had the pain and pleasure (painsure?) of be-friending them all.

One day, we all went to stay with the girl he was going

41

out with. She lived with her mum and dad in Hastings. She was very kind and upbeat, quite a straightforward girl from what I remember. She had a name like Clare or Emma. Clare Emma had aspirations to be a low-budget catalogue model. I say aspirations, she already heavily identified as a catalogue model (I added the low-budget). She self-identified as a model after appearing on a poster in a key cutter's window. Good old Clare – it's tough out there and she was genuinely a little piece of simple sunshine. Lord knows what she was doing knocking around with us lot. Kai once said of all his girlfriends she had been the best one because she was an actual model. And that is teen love in a nutshell.

◆ ◆ ◆

Thirteen was an impressionable age. My dad now had a wife called Kerry, who was way better than the Pontins' girlfriend. It must have been annoying for my mum that she did all the day-to-day boring stuff, like reprimanding us, and staying awake worrying about us, and there were we thinking my stepmum Kerry was cool because she smoked fags and wore Reebok Classics.

Although cracks were starting to appear in the relationship with my dad and Kerry. One Christmas, she didn't want to do the washing up, so she just threw all the plates away. I dare say there was a bit more to it than that – a statement – a domestic dance – I don't know,

I just heard about it secondhand. I remember thinking, WHAT A WASTE. I was often worried about waste.

We had a row when I was about thirteen because I cried about my dad drinking and nearly setting himself on fire and Kerry lost it – I think she had a lot going on – and she called me a 'snivelling little wretch'. I remember being quite shocked because I hadn't realised she didn't like me, or that I was doing anything wrong. But she did love my dad and I think everyone was in a mad old place.

I mean, case in point, shortly after this she stabbed my dad – she went for the heart but got the arm. I guess it's hard to get the heart when people are wiggling around. Obviously we were shocked and worried about Dad, who was fine after a small stay in A&E (God bless the NHS, etc.).

My first question was: 'Is Dad OK?' And then of course, my second question was: 'And what did he do to warrant the old stab?' And that's how I know I'm a feminist.

Even the most staunch feminist can fall in love at first sight with a MAN.

The Most Beautiful
Man in the Town

But even the most staunch feminist can fall in love at first sight with a MAN. Around this time I fell in love love, like LOVE, like love at first sight, for the first time.

A man walked past me one day and he was just impossibly beautiful: a tanned, muscly body that wasn't trying too hard, it just was. He had long brown hair that shone, it shone out because it belonged to the most beautiful head in the world. You'd shine, too, connected to that mainframe. He had big hands and the bluest eyes. You think you've seen good blue eyes before, heck, I've even seen them on a cat, but these were better because they were his. Truffle oil is good on its own, but with avocado and sourdough, it's a different league.

He had a strong lion's nose, as if he'd been a lion before, and he just brought the nose with him into this realm. You know, because he could. Because he was Lion Nose Man.

I felt positively sick, I stopped and just looked at him. And then I followed him. All the way home. Like an absolute nut job. I was just on autopilot. Having logged where he lived in my mind, a few days later I made my friend Gina come with me to call for him. This was back in the day, when you 'called' for someone. Granted, usually someone you knew.

So we knocked on the door, he opened it and there stood two strangers, two thirteen-year-old girls. In their school uniforms. Gina had bright orange hair and had yet to grow into her face or body, and I looked dyspraxic (probably was/am), I'd given myself a home perm and was suffering from some extremely bad acne.

He opened the door to see two unfortunate children and this is how the conversation went:

Him: 'Yeah?'

Me: 'Do you want to come to the park?'

Him: 'What for?'

Me: (Panicking, trying to be funny) 'I dunno. To fuck.'

Him: 'No, you're alright.'

Me: 'Haha. Cool, see ya.'

So yeah, I was a pretty cool kid.

Two years later, at the ripe old age of fifteen (big for

my age) and now with added clear skin,[2] I was down Louisa Bay, a pub in Broadstairs which I would later be barred from, but on the whole a gorgeous establishment. I was with some friends, snakebite and black in hand and I'd just popped a few songs on the jukebox. Pearl Jam, if I know me. And I turn around to see... Lion Nose. We lock eyes. A lightning bolt of electricity goes through me. He doesn't recognise me, of course he doesn't, I'm a different person: I'm Sandy after she gets the leather trousers.

The connection is instant and we hook up and I fall in love hard. Thankfully so does he. It's passionate, it's healing, it's intoxicating, it's everything. His face was like a sunset. It gave you hope. So long as it was there, the world would keep on turning.

I was fifteen, but I looked, acted and felt a lot older. I'd seen enough life. Plus, I lied to him about my age for a while.

We got into a relationship immediately and we were in many ways a match made in heaven, except he was too good-looking for me and it made me quite insecure. In our little town, there were these cool, beautiful twins. Yes, I grew up in Sweet Valley High. These twins (and you know I love twins) were insouciant, beautiful girls.

2   I took the acne treatment Roaccutane, which has had a bad press. People ask me, 'Did it make you depressed?' How would I know? I was fifteen, and already depressed. Better to be sad with good skin though.

Their dad owned all of the rides on the beach (boho chic), and one was AN ACTUAL MODEL! And more than just down at the local Timpsons. The other could have been a model if she wanted to – I think she was an artist, I don't know. I mean they were the town stars and he was just casually talking to them in the pub – no thank you.

Another day, a really beautiful surfer-type girl in the town left a note on his windscreen because she was so beguiled by him. So yeah, I was punching. It wasn't just his looks; his soul shone through. He looked like a man who could build his own house, or at least read *The Count of Monte Cristo* and make a nice vegetarian bolognese while he was doing it.

But even though he was the town prize, he didn't play games or make me feel insecure – he was a good guy, heart of a lion, nose of a lion. So what do I do? To this amazing man who had beautiful innards, who was fun, charismatic and a true piece of perfect? I cheat on him…

Loads. When I am so hammered, I sleep with people I don't care about who were not a patch on him. Why? Why? Why? I don't like to have regrets because I think we sometimes have to learn by making mistakes, but when you hurt people, when you scar a soul, you are making the world a more unpleasant place, so yes, that is one of my deepest regrets.

If I had to make excuses for past me (and there are

no excuses for cheating) I would say that part of me thought I didn't deserve him, and I did tend to be quite self-sabotaging at the time, but also part of me was just hedonistic and selfish.

The worst thing is I felt like my behaviour changed him. He trusted me and I broke a part of him. We are still friends to this day. We're not right for each other romantically now – we are so different, we'd drive each other bonko – but I'm very pleased he's in my life and I am very sad I ever betrayed him.

When I was younger, I didn't really think I could hurt men, because I didn't think they could actually love me. You forget that everyone else is also walking around with their own chinks.

A pig's head on a stick does not a party make.

A Dear
Pig's Ear

So yes, I was fast becoming a bit of a messer. Not a lot for my mum to show off about, but bless her, she gave it a good go anyhow. One summer, she was volunteering in a folk tent (hard brag) with a girl named Ruth. A folk tent is one of the tents they have in 'folk week' usually selling Aztec jewellery or knitted toilet roll holders. Now I guess you want me to tell you what folk week is? Well, some towns have a week devoted to folk music each year. And in this (difficult) time, you will see a lot more bearded men and old accordions knocking about.

Ruth is now a friend, but at the time she had just seen me around Broadstairs town: pissing in bus shelters, shouting at a drain, having sex in the bushes, your classic

51

small-town big-legend stuff. So Ruth's image of me was wildly different from the one my mum was portraying. My mum was saying things like, 'Lou bought a book the other week! Lou is thinking about eating more fruit! Lou said a phrase in German[3] the other day.'

Ruth heard my mum talking about her daughter Lou, and she visualised me stumbling about Thanet and thought, This woman must have two daughters named Lou. The only reasonable explanation… Well, if it works for George Foreman.[4]

There were things I managed to do that may have made my mum proud, though. Once in my secondary school I heard that the first-year kids were going to have a medieval banquet as part of their history lesson – good for them. But there was due to be a pig's head on a skewer, a sort of spit roast scenario.

Well, me and the other vegetarian, Kelly, KICKED OFF and said there was no need to glamorise such violence against animals. We made posters and put them up around the school. The headmaster called us into his office and said that we were ruining it for the first years, and some of them were crying because the school said they might cancel the whole thing.

~~~~~~~~~

3   *Swearword.

4   Yes, in case you didn't know, George Foreman of boxing and toastie grill fame called all five of his sons George and one of his daughters Georgetta. WOW! He ran out of ideas pretty quick.

Because two kids made a poster? How deranged and manipulative. You could just compromise, and get rid of the head. A pig's head on a stick does not a party make. Or just go ahead with the head. You don't need to threaten to cancel everything because two teenagers were expressing a difference of opinion. They should have been pleased with some dissonance; open it up for debate, it's interesting, put it to a vote. Don't shut down two kids for daring to discuss things.

Anyway, we had another meeting with the headmaster, and my mum said to go in and tell him that he's running an autocracy; she was all for us blustering around with our principles. I did just that, I marched in with my mother's defiance in me: 'Well, this is an autocracy.' Then he asked me what that meant. Ah. I hadn't thought this far. No idea. He'd got me.

But then we had the last laugh because the local paper got hold of the story. It must have been an extremely slow news week in Broadstairs because it was FRONT PAGE news. It read: 'Dane Court School makes a Pig's Ear of Things'. The school were really cross, Kelly and I thought it was brilliant, but we admitted to each other, privately, that neither of us reported it to the paper, we wished we did, but alas. I am pretty sure my mum was behind it, so actually it's me who is proud of her.

**Trousers down,
covered in sick.
Hello?
Is it me you're
looking for?**

Apologies to the Babysitter and Tents Aren't Soundproof

By fifteen, my friends and I were all pissheads and we loved sculling Mad Dog 20/20 or super-strength beer on the way to the pub. I lived for getting smashed. It was my escape, I loved to numb myself and sink below thoughts and feelings.

Often I was told I was a 'different kind of drunk' and I hated it. I resented a stranger seeing through me in one night. People judging me was bad enough but my real concern was that if I couldn't drink normally, people would try and take alcohol away from me. That was too sad to contemplate.

One night I got so obliterated in the local pub,

I couldn't walk home. I remember these two guys walking me up the hill because I was staggering and swaying too much. God bless them, they dropped me off, all of us wobbling up the hill.

When I remember this, I can see the picture of it but as an observer, so my point of view is above, looking down at me and the other two men. That's weird, but hey, I'm not a psychologist.

I was staggering back because I was due to be relieving my little brother's babysitter (oh yeah, my Stepdad and Mum had a kid together by the way). I met this babysitter at the beginning of the night, I had seen her around the town, quite a serious girl, probably an A-grade student. Why not, I guess. If you can get an A you'd be silly not to. Anyway, the deal was that I would take over from her at 10 p.m., so my parents could stay out at a folk club (you know they were big on that by now) and they wouldn't have to shell out for a sitter into the night. Makes sense, but what actually happened is I turned up at gone eleven and fell through the door, ran to the loo upstairs, accidentally locked myself in, and couldn't get out. I was then promptly sick into my pubes, shouted at the girl to 'fucking fuck off and just fucking fuck off' and then passed out on the toilet. Small town, big legend indeed.

The babysitter had never seen a display of 'art' like this – sheltered life much, love? No, of course it wasn't ideal for the nice lady, so she called the pub that my mum and stepdad were in and told the bar staff to find them and tell them they needed to come home for an emergency. They went into absolute panic mode, as you would. They thought something had happened to my little brother and so they flagged down a passing police car for a lift.

When they got there, they must have been relieved it was just me being a moron. My mum catastrophises a lot, and imagines the worst, but once she's face to face with a genuine problem, she often goes very calm. The biggest example of this is when my stepdad died. My mum heard him breathing in his sleep, and it sounded irregular and odd. She then heard him take what would have been his last breath. She remained calm, phoned 999, lifted him onto the floor, and tried to bring him back to life. From the way she tells it, I think she was very present and very calm, folding into the moment. No hysterics, for fear that it would make the outcome worse. She's brave and incredible like that.

Obviously this story is in a different arena, stress-wise, but again, she kept her head. She had to try and talk me out of the bathroom and slowly explain how to use the lock. I do remember just staring at it, a lock I'd used thousands of times, and thinking, Yep, that's a bit of a puzzle. I couldn't quite muster the energy and coordination needed to pull it across half an inch from right to left. She repeated the instructions a few times until I managed to do it. But I'm not a hero! I'm just a girl whose mum figured out the lock!

I opened the door to her, trousers down, covered in sick. Hello? Is it me you're looking for?

The next day I was grounded for about two months. I said I was going to give up drinking and learn the guitar. I didn't really manage either of those things but I wish I did. I'd love to be able to play the guitar now. But the guitar didn't quiet my mind in the way I was convinced that the booze did.

I remember bumping into the babysitter years later and I was sober at the time (one of the sobriety stints that lasted a few months). And I remember her saying to me, 'I will always remember you, because no matter how bad life got, I thought, well, at least I'm not that girl.'

Delighted I could be of service! Blessings come in mysterious ways!

Around this time, pre-GCSEs and pre-moving out, the clashes with my stepdad were getting worse. My older brother had already left home at sixteen because he'd chased him out. And now my brother had gone, my stepdad was doing more and more perplexing things to me.

One time my mum said I could go to London to stay with my boyfriend (Lion Nose) for two nights if I promised to call their house phone at 6 p.m. on the dot each night to say I was safe. I did this both nights and made my stepdad write it down because I wanted my mum to know I was OK, and that I could be trusted to do what I had promised. I knew it was important to her.

He didn't tell her I had called and when she asked if I had, he said, 'No, she hasn't, which is typically selfish of her.' But *he* was the one being selfish and worrying my mum. I didn't even know he'd done this until I got back and she asked why I hadn't called.

Things like this made me feel like I was going insane. Up until then I thought adults behaved like adults, but I was starting to see that really they were as fucked up as a school bully. It seemed like a worse betrayal though, because they were supposed to protect you.

My mum didn't do much about it, or maybe she felt like she didn't want to address it, because the repercussions would be too big for her. I get why she didn't feel strong enough to confront it, but I was left feeling very isolated and like I couldn't trust anyone. With hindsight, I do now think he was just an unconscious man, terrified of losing my mum. I am not excusing it, or negating the impact, but maybe he was just acting from fear because he couldn't access love.

And the potential autism wouldn't have helped. We all joked about his autism, and even he once said, 'Do you know, I did a test for autism once and I was very bloody good at it.' I think he'd done an online test, but he never bothered to get a formal diagnosis.

One of the worst times we clashed was another camping holiday in France. I really didn't want to come because things were already frayed, to say the least. So on this holiday, it was just my mum, my stepdad, my half-brother, and my friend Helena. My mum had said it would look bad if I didn't come, so she let me bring a friend – lovely stuff, well played me. I don't know who it would look bad to, the neighbours I assume, but I think they would have had bigger things to worry about than whether I went to the Dordogne or not.

Initially, I was getting on with my stepdad – having a laugh – and I thought, this is nice, finally we are getting on. I felt a warm glow in my heart. Things were harmonious in the Dordogne.

He then went into the tent and said to my mum, 'Oh Louise is being absolutely vile,' and went on to absolutely INVENT an entire scene that did not happen. Like an impassioned improviser. I couldn't believe my little ears. Also, he was supposed to be a smart man and he was doing this in a raised voice IN A TENT. Of course I could hear him. It wasn't a magic tent.

I walked in and said, 'Why are you doing this? This is all utter lies and you know it.' He panicked and bluffed and stuck to his guns, like an MP. My mum looked crushed. She knew I was telling the truth. It's hard when someone is a good husband, except in one area. Big area though, to be fair, your own kids.

He stormed out of the tent, and I was shaking but had to find out more. I followed after him, I was so hurt and confused. I just asked him, 'Why, why are you doing this, I don't understand, we were getting on?'

And he said, 'Because you are vulgar, repulsive and you repel me.'

He didn't have to love me but why did he hate me? I didn't hate him. Why was I hateable? I cleaned up after myself, I asked how everyone was, I tried to keep things light – I just wanted everyone to be happy.

'But I'm not a bad person, you know that,' I said, 'because I have nice friends and you like them, so why can't you just like me?'

He said, 'I have no idea why you have such nice friends.'

I said, 'But I do have friends and they like me. And you don't have any friends.'

I didn't like saying that to him, because at the time it was true. I felt cruel, but I was trying to make him and myself realise that maybe I'm not the only problem here.

Shortly after this holiday, I moved out. I was fifteen. I felt mad with the politics in the house. My stepdad had got rid of my brother and now me, he just did not want us there. What I wish we had known then was that his behaviour wasn't really about us as people. I think it was just that he was obsessed with bloodlines and we weren't his children. Like an animal in the wild stamping out threats, it was primal to him. Once we were out of his house, through time, he was able to get to know us as people and start to love us.

I was drinking a lot to try and stop myself from feeling so much. I was also making myself sick and binge eating a lot. And I just felt genuinely unhinged.

I was only able to move out because I found a charity who helped people sign on early if they had irrevocable differences at home – I don't know how I found them. Serendipity? Luck? The woman running it was so supportive and understanding. Thank God for her, a benefits system, and a bit of cash-in-hand work. I believe very few people want to be on benefits forever, and if they really do then good luck to them because that's not a great life. Benefits are a lifeline for some people and I think they should be raised so that people can breathe (and eat) while they contemplate and gather strength for their next steps.

I told my mum I had to move out because I was going insane. She knew I was bulimic and had a drink problem, and she did try to talk to me about it. I think it made her very sad and anxious and she felt like she'd failed. But I don't know what she could have done. She couldn't put us both first.

Before I left, I did pluck up the guts to ask her one day,

'Mum, why don't you just leave him because he hates us and causes so much trouble?'

She said, 'Because you will go away and leave home and then I'll have no one.' I appreciated the honesty at least.

Looking back, I am so glad she didn't kick him out. He was faithful to her and I didn't have to worry about her because she had him. It's funny how life works out, because in later life, she unleashed a stream of constant low-level daily gripes on him, so karma comes out one way or another. I actually felt for him then, it was too much too late really. But that's their business.

Anyway, I was all set up to go. I explained to Mum there was a scheme that would help me do it and I would be moving about five minutes' walk away and she could come and see me whenever she wanted. I said I would work hard on my GCSEs, but it would be easier this way.

She was really cross. I don't know if she thought I would spiral, but she didn't say she was worried about me. She mainly focused on how bad it looked to the neighbours. I guess shame runs deep. I said I didn't care about that – if they asked, she could tell them what she wanted, they were Christians anyhow, so it's in the handbook not to judge! I just had to go. She said, 'Well, because I don't approve of it, you are not taking anything like your duvet or any saucepans. I'm not helping you do this because I don't agree with it.'

I do understand, I mean the last thing my mum wanted at this stage was the neighbours to see me with a duvet on my back, trotting down the road, pretending to be a snail.

But I didn't care. I didn't care at all. I was free. And it wasn't so I could get drunk or come in late. I did that anyway. As soon as I walked away from the house, I felt my brain and body fog clearing. I didn't have to live under a roof where so many games were being played, and I didn't understand the rules. I went down to Woolworths and bought the cheapest duvet and pillows. Never mind covers, that could wait. So long as I had the basics I would be very happy indeed.

Don't let the jean cut-downs throw you off the scent.

Forgiving My Stepdad

Forgiving my stepdad didn't happen overnight, it was a gradual process. I was angry at my parents for some years – who isn't?

Aged eighteen, nineteen, twenty, I would sometimes try to get an apology from him and ask why he did certain things, but he didn't remember, or didn't want to. So I went off to do the work on my own.

I started to try and see the bigger picture. He wasn't used to the kind of child I was: noisier, less focused and more emotional. I was quite full-on, I would leave love letters for my family all the time, and tell everyone how lucky we were because water came out of the tap! And that 'in Africa they had to walk for miles for water'. I mean that's a bold statement, missing a lot of geographical precision, but I was seven.

When I had been living at home, most of his wages were going into a household of three kids, two of whom were not biologically his. I can see how that would grate on someone. More biccies to buy!

In my twenties, I realised he was a limited man of a certain age. And they were really fucked over. They weren't allowed to express emotions, so naturally at some point there could be an avalanche of the stuff coming down in all directions.

As he aged, he lent into a softness and an honesty that was beautiful and made him powerful in a much deeper way. He also became more and more selfless. He didn't want a lot for himself. He refused birthday and Christmas presents and would tell us, instead, to buy a goat for a village. Usually a village that would need a goat; he wasn't just sending a ram up to Milton Keynes for a laugh.

I was less of a threat, too: the more I went away and lived my own life, the more he felt safe in his. Once he knew I wasn't going to marry my mum or turn her against him, we grew closer. You can choose to see someone's good points, for an easier life. And I think we both did that with each other. I guess we are all carrying our own battle scars around and trying to defend our territory as best we can. No one sets out to cause pain unless they are loaded up with the stuff themselves.

As I got older, I could see that even though his

behaviour towards me felt personal, it probably wasn't, because he was so offensive to EVERYONE. One example that I sometimes chuckle about is when my Uncle Quentin came to visit my parents one Christmas.

Now, Quentin is my mum's brother and is everyone's favourite family member. He's the type of guy who still gets out library books, makes a jumper last twenty years and will enrol in a night class to learn about the migration habits of the Blackpoll Warbler just because he knows everything else. My stepdad loved him, I love him, we all love him.

Quentin turns up, a near seventy-year-old who has just driven four hours on Christmas Day. He rings the doorbell. My stepdad answers the door and barks: 'OH BLOODY HELL, IT'S YOU IS IT, QUENTIN? WELL, THIS IS NOT A CONVENIENT TIME, NOT A CONVENIENT TIME AT ALL.' And lets the door shut in his face.

Merry Christmas one and all! An hour later, wine in hand, we're all chortling away about it.

As he aged, my stepdad did make more and more friends, people really liked him. He could be curmudgeonly, but he knew that was when he was at his funniest. He loved making people laugh and would sell himself down the river to do it. Really he was a big softie with a liberal heart and the older he got, the more he let people see it; he relaxed into life. He would tip his head back and roar with laughter. Quite often at his own jokes,[5] but we adored it and he would fill the room with ridiculousness.

Once he came to a small comedy show of mine in Margate and he gave me notes live during the show; we heckled each other with love, joy and a bit of bloody good humour.

Before he retired he taught at an all-girls' private school and a lot of the students adored him. They were quite protective of him and he was very touched that they thought he was a 'legend'. I think it's because he was himself, he would swear, he would slag off what he didn't agree with, and he would roll his eyes dramatically around his head. And in some ways, that's quite novel.

The first turning point between us came a few months after I had moved out. I came back to their house to open my GCSE results. He put such gravity on education and he was pretty sure I had flunked them all. When my results turned out to be quite good, he was as surprised as he was elated. He saw that I wasn't a complete write-off and I saw that he did somehow care about my future. We both respected each other a tiny bit more after that. Something to build on.

When I used to go home in my twenties, I gravitated towards my mum. We tried not to exclude him but he didn't want to have a look at the tops in Peacocks.

---

5 Maybe we had more in common than we thought.

My mum loved it when I came home and while he was a bit envious that she lit up, he also liked to see her happy.

Some of my favourite memories are from a few years ago when he, my mum and I would attempt a crossword. All bickering along the way, me thick as a brick and sometimes Mumma holding back so I could get it. Heaven.

To have them still alive and healthy when I was in my late thirties was marvellous and when I was with them I would drink them in and say, 'We are SO LUCKY' and he'd say, 'For God's sake, Louise, you're always saying that, do shut up.' Yin and yang! Having fun in our own way.

During the lockdown, my mum was convinced my stepdad had Parkinson's, and we told her she was just finding something else to worry about as we'd already dealt with a few phantom worries. And then he got the diagnosis. Super annoying for her #believeheretc.

He tried to get used to shuffling along and hated that people had to wait for him. He took it in his stride, it was just a way shorter stride. Seeing him teeter on steps, and try to style it out, that was tough. Seeing the Parkinson's start to ravage him was heartbreaking.

He would often surprise you with his jokes, sometimes dark or risqué, sometimes bonkers! Once I brought a boyfriend home and we went to see a Tracey Emin exhibition in Margate. Before long, the four of us had come face to face with a picture that said: 'Is anal sex legal?' To break the ice, my stepdad leant into my new boyfriend and said, 'If it is illegal, I've broken the law a few times!', which he followed with a cheeky wink. This was made worse only by the fact he was dressed in denim hot pants at the time. I know what you're thinking... this is off brand for the man you have got to know, but they were just jeans he turned into shorts and my mum had snipped too much off. Well, if you've got it, flaunt it!

He got looser in his later years too, even agreeing to let me take him to a white witch in Thanet. I had taken my mum to see her with glorious results and I wanted to treat my stepdad too, even though I knew it wasn't really his thing. My mum and I often did things together and I didn't want him to feel left out. And I thought it might be good for him as he faced mortality. I think he mainly went to keep me and Mum happy, but also out of intrigue. And it probably helped that we told him the white witch was stunning.

By this time the Parkinson's had really set in, so he found moving hard, but he was adamant he would get down onto the floor himself to lie on the crystal bed and get back up again. It took him about five minutes but he did it.

When I collected him after his appointment, I asked how he found it. He smiled and shook his head as if he was on the brink of a lifetime's epiphany and said,

'Do you know, I don't think I am really that much of a spiritual person.' And we laughed and drove home. I was touched that we accepted each other's worlds, even if we didn't fully understand them.

He also did a lot for Amnesty International, hated corruption, and wrote lots of letters to the local paper. But one of my favourite letters he wrote was to a brewery in Thanet who had their pub decorated in Krays' memorabilia. The Kray brothers used to frequent the pub, and the pub thought this was a cool connection, so they had pictures of them up in the pub and a few newspaper articles about them. Local celebrities. Very aspirational!

Anyhow, my stepdad wrote the brewery a letter detailing some of the things these KRAYzeee brothers did to people. Gruesome stuff, gorgeous letter. Not sure if he included piccies, but it was a fairly long piece detailing their graphic torture with a blow-by-blow account of some of the violent acts. Then, before he anonymously signed off, he asked the beer house if that was the sort of thing they wanted to encourage. They took all of the memorabilia down.

Acceptance and letting go is the most powerful thing you can do (outside of legal action of course).

Destruction 101

In the grittier days, back before the resolution between me and my stepdad, I carved out my own little space and things in my flat were pretty good in their own way. I had the refuge of Lion Nose and we were hanging out all of the time. We both had the same hobby and passion that ignited us – boozing.

After some time we decided to move in together and thought we would start again in a new, bigger flat that we both rented. We found a place at the bottom of the hill in Broadstairs, spacious, near the sea and super-cheap.

There was a slight catch: you had to walk through a fish yard to get in. So we would jump over puddles of blood and floating fish heads to get home, but when you're young, skint and in love you can tolerate these things.

I loved living with Lion Nose, although we'd been

dating for a year and a half, so the romance was waning, or at least changing, as these things do. It wasn't bad, but I missed the intoxication he'd had for me initially, so I was scared he would abandon me. I think sometimes if you are scared of something happening you almost bring it into being because you are giving it so much energy. And eventually we did split up, a year later. Although mainly because of my aforementioned cheating.

I wish that this period had been different. I ruined it all by being so drunk and cheating on him. Horrible, terrible, regrettable. He was the good thing in my life and I self-destructed. Although looking back now, there were rifts and I think both of us probably needed to separate, but neither was brave enough.

My drinking at this time, especially after the break-up, was through the roof. I moved out and got a place with my brother and painted the flat bright orange (a cry for help, surely) and perhaps just as worryingly, I was hiding vodka bottles under the bed at this time. I actually tried to make my own vodka in this flat – entrepreneurial or desperate, you decide. Anyway, my homeless friend Greg drunk it all while it was black and in the fermentation stage.

My friend Jules was a good influence in my life and was a lot calmer than me and some of my other friends. She'd helped me with my science GCSEs and was smart and funny. One day she just lost it at me and said she couldn't hang around with me and see me drinking like this, it wasn't cool and she wanted no part of it.

Of course drinking was a stronger urge than friendship at the time, and I had plenty of people who would indulge me. So I blamed her for not being 'fun' and we drifted apart for years. What a solid friend to call this out; it's hard at that age to stand up for what you think is right, and I am so glad she did. While I couldn't stop drinking then, all these warnings soak into the fabric of your soul for when you are strong enough to change.

◆ ◆ ◆

I was so devastated to split up with Lion Nose, I was in pieces. My Aunty Sue knew I was sad and she wanted someone to go on holiday with, so my dear old aunty bought us plane tickets and booked a hostel in Alicante. The only issue being that Aunty Sue didn't have six months left on her passport and you do need that. So we queued up for our flight and she wasn't allowed to board with me, she had to turn back round and try and get an expedited passport, so she wouldn't be flying out for a couple of days. Maybe I should have stayed with her, but she was insistent that I go ahead. She was kind like that.

However, we hadn't thought of getting to the hostel. When I got there I realised all I had was the name of the hostel and I spoke no Spanish. I got to the city and asked a few people and no one had any clue what I was talking about. I was shooting in the dark, hoping for the best, with very little money; I was a bit effed. I was just wandering around with a little suitcase looking lost and asking people if they'd heard of a hostel that could have been anywhere on the 200-kilometre-squared of Alicante.

Eventually, a very nice couple felt sorry for me and said I was a similar age to their daughter and took me in for the night and we all ate a meal together. It was incredibly generous and I could not believe how gracious they were. The next day they found and dropped me at the hostel, saying their daughter would bring some friends and meet me in the bar that night since she would be back from university and I was on my own. The whole luscious, generous family might have regretted that after what followed next.

In preparation for my new friend's arrival, I drank almost a litre of vodka. I'd bought the bottle to save money and have a few before I went out, but also for Dutch courage. I thought I would just have a few, but I was gulping it down. I distinctly remember looking at this litre bottle of Smirnoff Blue Label, and I thought, Oh hang on, I've drunk nearly all of this, in just over an hour. I don't think that's good, and yet I feel fine. Hero much?

As soon as I left my room to go downstairs and meet my new Spanish friends, the air, the movement, and I dare say the alcohol must have HIT ME AND HIT ME HARD because I don't remember a lot after that. I think

I collapsed, but I couldn't tell you how I know that. I remember ambulance lights and that's about it. I'm not sure what happened, because it was in the days before anyone could film it for TikTok, and not surprisingly, the Spanish family didn't stay in touch with shared anecdotes of the night.

What I do remember is waking up in hospital and my vision, my thinking, well, my everything, feeling very blurred. I was slow to move, and I wasn't in my body. I had sick all down me and a nurse was just looking at me with a smirk on his face.

I asked him what happened and he said, 'Stomach pumpeee' and did a pumping gesture. I said, 'I know but what else, what else happened?' He just shrugged – he didn't want to communicate and seemed to find the whole thing to his amusement.

He communicated when he wanted to, though, because later when it was time to discharge me, he asked me where I was going now, and this time I had a card from the hostel with the address on. He said he would give me a lift. I was a walking zombie. I was just putting one foot in front of the other. And he was manoeuvring me towards his car.

I must have thought it's cool how Alicante is so small that the nurse can just drop an idiotic English girl home and free up the bed, what a nice end-to-end service. He stopped by a building and I just sat in the car, but he said we needed to go and get something, so I trudged after him. We went into what I came to realise was his flat and he pushed me on the sofa, removed my trousers, put on a condom and had sex with me. I didn't put up a fight. I wish I had, I really wish I had punched him square in the face, but I guess I just thought this is what I deserve. This is all I am, a shell. I was numb. I wasn't moving and I had sick down my front, he couldn't have thought I was there from choice. I guess he thought I was nothing and he could do what he wanted, and I guess part of me unconsciously agreed.

Looking back, I am so sad for that girl and millions like her. Previously, I always lamented my part in this; why didn't I shout, why didn't I resist and fight, why didn't I at least try to reason with this man? I now know it's because I had just come round and didn't have the energy and wherewithal or confidence to challenge someone way older and bigger than me, in authority, in his country, in a different language.

There was a hopelessness to it, sinking into such a sad fate. But it still always nagged away at my subconscious and my soul.

Then recently, I talked to a therapist about it and she said maybe I was protecting myself. He had the cold calculations and the dead-eyed stare of a complete psychopath, so maybe, instinctively, I gave him one thing so that he didn't take more. This resonated and it made me feel better. It could have been worse.

I wonder how many people he's done that to, people in his 'care'. For him to temporarily escape his demons, he dents someone else's spirit and becomes a blight on their life. Is it worth it to ejaculate?

When my Aunty Sue got there later that day I told her what happened, with the stomach pumping, but not the dead-eyed nurse. I had put that into the deep recesses of my mind to forget about, with all the other unpleasant stuff. It was locked away in a safe for now, a safe containing the opposite of treasures.

She was very kind to me but gently suggested I had a drink problem. I was pretty sure I was too young for a drink problem, thank you. I just misjudged it, it was more of a timing thing, and I was just sad right now, so drinking more than usual. I didn't drink that night, but the next night I was back on wine with dinner at least, to help me blot out the start of the holiday.

Through therapy, healing and meditation, I've let go of the resentment towards this guy. I had to. Resentment means to re-feel and I wanted to take back control. He hurt me once, but it was up to me how long I let him go on hurting me. Acceptance and letting go is the most powerful thing you can do (outside of a legal action, of course).

Let's just enjoy the story, knowing that no one got hurt and I have never and will never do it again.

When Life Gives You Lemons, Drink Lemongrass

Back in Broadstairs sometime later, I got myself into another little scrape. I never used to drink-drive, except for this one time when that's exactly what I did. Which was crazy because the police knew my car.

My car was purchased for £200 – the exact money I got in inheritance from my stepdad's grandparents who were absolutely lush. There was some discussion as to whether or not me and my brother should have the money as we were not blood relatives, but seeing as they treated us as equals and we all seemed to love each other equally, and IT WAS IN THE FUCKING WILL, they let us have it.

WHAT'S THAT LADY DOING?

It was a red mini with a number plate featuring OGGY. At the time, my friend's boyfriend worked in a graphic design place, so said he would decorate my car in a surprise way for a laugh; I handed it over immediately. He was going to go with fire flames, but thankfully he went with Spider-Man on the bonnet and roof so it looked like he was climbing up the car. Good stuff.

There was a policeman around Thanet who stopped and gave me a producer every time he saw me, some sort of weird power game. Once he even tried to push my car down a hill to test the handbrake, he was such a little weirdo. When I stopped driving he did exactly the same thing to another young girl.

I should explain what a producer is. If a police officer gave you a producer, it just meant you had to bring your insurance, MOT and driving licence into the police station within a certain time frame. I was always popping in with my documents, and no one questioned it, in fact he got other officers to pull me over too, and one day I got TWO producers.

So they all knew me, so drink driving would be crazy, and yet here we are… Now, we all know that operating a car under the influence of any substance is incredibly stupid, selfish and deplorable, but I was seventeen and drunk, so let's just enjoy the story, knowing that no one got hurt and I have never and will never do it again.

It was about midnight and I had my friend Katy

with me. At some point we figured that the police were trailing us, so I thought I would throw them off the scent by travelling about eight miles an hour. Very clever. But weirdly, they were still on our tail… the slowest police chase ever.[6]

Then I thought, Right, time for me to really fox them. And so I indicated left, but I turned right! Yep – deal with that rozzers! These guys must have been top of their game, because they still caught up with me and made me pull over.

Don't worry I HAD ONE MORE TRICK UP MY SLEEVE. I had some lemongrass aromatherapy oil in my car, so I drunk that. I think to disguise the alcohol. Now, I'm not a scientist, but Katy was chucking around the idea of sucking on coppers (the coins, not the men in uniform), however we didn't have any change, so I went down the less trodden, lemongrass route.

The policeman got me out of the car and started to arrest me on suspicion of drink-driving. He was speaking into a Dictaphone with a Partridge-esque voice and said, 'On arresting the subject proceeded to drink [looks at the label] half a bottle of lemongrass aroma-therapy oil.'

So off we popped to the police station in Margate (we took his car in the end), and I said goodbye to Katy.

---

6 Incidentally, this would be a nice scene in a film – we've seen all the fast ones, time for something new!

At the police station, I don't think there was a lot going on, so all the coppers crowded around me and were having a go. It was honestly about five men and one hard-looking woman circling me. A different time of course, as nowadays you wouldn't find so many on the same shift. Obviously I was totally to blame, but I was a bit annoyed that they were all piling in on me, so I started to play up. The conversation went a bit like this:

Me: 'I know I'm fit but it doesn't need all of you to arrest me.'

Them: 'This is very serious what you've done.'

Me: 'I actually don't find the uniform sexy, so you're wasting your time.'

Them: 'You could have killed someone on the road tonight – my daughter could have been on the road.'

Me: 'At ten miles an hour, seems unlikely. I'm really enjoying your company here, but surely one or two of you should go and check on some other crime.'

Them: 'You know that everything you say is being filmed by the cameras up there and we can read it out in a court of law.'

Me: 'Well, bring out the DVD, baby!'

Them: (Leading me to the desk) 'OK, do you want a lawyer?'

Me: (Slamming my fist on the desk in a cartoon way) 'I want the best in town, baby!'

Them: 'You're on benefits, correct?'

Me: 'Yes.'

Then there was some talk about a free lawyer and I was shoved in a cell for the night and they refused to bring me a blanket even though I was in a vest top and freezing all night. So I guess they won.

When it came to the ruling, the lawyer assigned to me had a chat with me for about fifteen minutes before we entered the court – that was the first time I met him and I swear to God when we were talking, he got a boner. Isn't that so odd? Maybe his power was in his extended rod, because I was lucky to get a £250 fine and a ban for two years. I had gone off driving anyhow.

As I was leaving the police cell the next morning, the bleak realisation of what I had done set in. I called my mum to explain, bracing myself for a showdown. At this time in her life, my mum was mid-way through the first term of a counselling course (which she sadly didn't continue) and with this new perspective, she said, 'That was a silly thing you did but I don't love you any less.'

Because she had been so nice, I felt worse and vowed to never ever do it again. The responsibility fell firmly at my feet to not be an asshole. It was easier to try and raise myself up because someone had my back and someone believed I could be better than a worm.

Shame makes you feel like you are infected and

there's nothing you can do so you are destined to destroy everything, whereas she gave me the dignity of recognising it was a mistake and not who I was at my core.

When you judge someone else, you're just judging yourself — and that's a spiritual law, babe.

(Sung)

Being on the Passenger Side of the Older Guys' Rides

Just after this, still about seventeen I think, I started sleeping with a man over forty. A guy who, excuse the cliché, had just split up with his wife.

One of my best mates at the time, and still now (lucky me) was Helena. You'll remember her from the Dordogne of course. Helena (or Hels to me): so tall, so thin, so ginger, we called her the giraffe – yes, I guess we were creative even back then. Actually, she gave the nickname to herself. Hels was so laid-back and so goddam cute and cool. She still is (lucky her).[7]

---

7   At the time of writing.

She'd just sort of lope around, only eat what she wanted AND LEAVE THE REST – very chic if you ask me. I was still eating everything and secretly yakking it back up. Much more Parisian not to need it. She enjoyed it, she would graze or gorge depending on how hungry she was and then simply push her plate away, not giving it a second chance. Nonchalant around cake. Beggars belief.

Hels was not only very fun to be around, she also never bothered judging anyone. She'd just chuckle away and roll around. Lazy as fuck, mind you, loved being horizontal. Maybe she wasn't eating enough. With everything – men, food, nights out – she always knew when it was enough. Patted her tum, giggled away and laid down in the taxi home.

I was more 'on'. I couldn't watch a film without flicking through the Yellow Pages at the same time, and I was a tiny bit judgy, which I detest. But when you judge someone else, you're just judging yourself – and that's a spiritual law, babe. I'm learning not to be, so I can't even judge myself for this now, or it's part of the same problem. Judge Loulie!

So Helena was seeing this forty-something's friend. Two forty-plus-year-olds and two seventeen-year-olds. We must have looked bananas. Not at first glance, of course. At first glance it would have looked very sweet – two dads and their daughters. Hang on. That man's just grabbed his daughter's arse. That's weird. Is that a Ramsgate thing?

Helena's guy was better-looking (obviously), he had the long hair and the sports car (don't shy away from a totally trad mid-life crisis). My guy had short hair, and I was going to describe him, but I'm sorry to say he was awfully nondescript. Short brown hair. Ordinary clothes. Black jeans, normal build, so, so plain. Not my type at all, but I wasn't going to let that stand in the way of something to do.

We felt a bit weird about the age difference and we certainly didn't want our parents to find out – but we knew exactly what was going on. Well, we felt like we did at the time, and we were getting what we wanted out of the deal. We got free lifts, dinners and drinks. I'm not seeing the seventeen-year-olds picking up the bill for a plate of nachos and twenty piña coladas at Los Iguanas.

We knew they were wrong 'uns, but we thought we held the power, and we knew we'd skip off soon enough. Not that I was consciously engaging with what we were doing, but we didn't want anything serious and we didn't take them seriously.

We didn't have feelings for these men, they couldn't hurt us, and we had already had sex with other people. I actually lost my virginity before Lion Nose to a lovely man who really cared about me and wrote me poetry.

Naturally, I finished with him. Side note: I am sure I was way more popular with guys when I treated them really badly. Maybe I was just younger, drunker and less picky.

Anyway, back to these old pervs... we were so YOUNG and they must have felt weird as heck cavorting around with us. None of us fitted each other, we were just wasting time, finding something new to get a kick out of and bury our scars in. I'm pretty sure we would laugh about the situation, but somewhere in my body it gave me the ick.

In slight defence of these guys (Stockholm syndrome much) we were mature for our age, very independent, we thought we knew everything and we cared about nothing. But did we just *think* we were adults? It's hard to say, we couldn't have looked older than nineteen, which is still far too young for men over thirty, let alone over forty.

Helena reminded me that her fella did fall asleep on the job, at least once. She thought he was pranking her but no, there he was, out sparko, snoring away. As for me and my seasoned spectacle, one night when I was messing around with him in his bedroom (dick stuff, I'm sure), his daughter walked in. Don't worry, it's OK, because SHE WENT TO THE SAME SCHOOL AS ME. Mind you, that's not my shame, or hers, I am laying that firmly at her daddy's door. And even then, I dare say he was going through some kind of breakdown. Not ideal. I remember at the time, though, me and my friends found it pretty funny.

You might think I'm being very flippant about all this – I know now it's gross o'clock in Wrongsville USA – but that's how we were. Was I carefree or numb? Hard to say – a bit of both I think. I do have a recollection of turning up at my parents' house in Canterbury (yes, they had moved, well done for keeping track). The guy and I had got stranded and had to stay the night. Imagine that, me and a man double my age rat-a-tat-tatting on Mother and Father's door for a bed for the night. And we both STAYED THE NIGHT, separate rooms, sure. But just me, him and my parents. When we arrived, my mum had a horrified look in her eyes and pulled me aside: 'Louise, please tell me you are not sleeping with that man' – and I said, 'NOOOOO' and felt hot shame coursing through my body. So, yes, like in many situations my body knew it was off kilter before I did.

◆ ◆ ◆

I didn't like that I had a reputation around the town of being a drunk, I had a lot of shame about the things I'd done. So I dealt with that by drinking. Therefore what I was doing instead of sedating the shame was multiplying it.

Shame doesn't motivate change, quite the opposite.

You think that is who you are, so you double down, a lost cause. It doesn't matter what you do, the shame snake is in you.

It's much healthier to see yourself as a lovable person capable of good and bad decisions. Then you can more likely correct your path and make better choices.

I'm glad young people generally drink less now, it's a good sign that they might be able to process things more. I've got a lot of faith in this new lot really. Think they're popping out more evolved, which makes sense really.

If you want your boss to pay for your taxi home from work, just get so drunk that they absolutely have to.

The Worst Bartender in Margate

A t seventeen[8] I was working as a bartender in one of the roughest pubs in Margate. The crowd was a mix of people who had been barred from other establishments, people with electronic tags on their ankle, and some of the area's most unusual concubines. It was full of lost souls. As the old saying goes, like attracts like. It was run by a couple called Pam and Bob and they, as you can imagine, had seen all sorts. The establishment let you accept drinks from customers while you worked. Big mistake, Pam and Bob, big mistake.

One night, I'd had some super-strength lager on the

8   And yes, I did lie about my age again.

bus over, so the double whiskies really topped off the trouble. By 10 p.m., I had burnt the arm of my jumper, I had one foot stuck in the bounteous fag bin, and I had smashed a whole dishwasher tray full of drinks into a wall. I was not winning any bar staff awards that night and of course, I got asked to leave. It turns out, if you want your boss to pay for your taxi home from work, just get so drunk that they absolutely have to.

Later on I found out that I was so wasted my bosses thought that I couldn't have just been intoxicated – I must have been on drugs. I was not on drugs – well, not that night anyhow. I was too humiliated to call up to see if I had lost my job, but let's assume I had, I mean they weren't ringing me to say that they missed me.

I know you might think pull yourself together, stop drinking, stop getting into trouble, but when you are empty and you don't know how to fill yourself up, you just keep doing the same thing.

Also when you are lost and broken, people know they can use and abuse you, so your strength is depleted through more unfortunate events, and it becomes harder and harder to get help. You feel like you're dissolving.

It's hard to forgive if you don't know what you're forgiving, it's hard to accept if you don't know what you're accepting.

Rape is a Four-letter Word

One Friday night, I got in a taxi from Ramsgate to Broadstairs at about 2 a.m. My friends were waiting for me at someone's house. The journey takes about ten minutes. This one took me an hour and I did not pick up my phone, so I had lots of missed calls, which was very unusual for me.

When I finally arrived, they asked me what happened and why I took so long. I had no idea. I could remember getting in the taxi and getting out of it, but nothing in between. How weird is that? Plus, my top was ripped and I had a massive red mark on my back, in the shape, weirdly, of an iron. It wasn't a burn but it was big and red and lasted for about a week and we could not figure out what it was.

I have no idea what happened but I felt sick and I knew it wasn't good. My memory had blanked it out, or something darker had happened, or both. I am pretty sure the driver didn't date-rape me with Rohypnol, as those effects apparently last longer. It seems dramatic to think he would chloroform me but *something* happened. I was so perturbed about my memory being removed from the journey it frightened and angered me.

I was so incensed and confused that I did actually phone up the taxi rank the next day (I think they were called Happy Taxis, ironically, and they've changed their name now, but they are in the same place and I think about it every time I walk by them). I called and said I needed to know who the cab driver was. I told them all the details, so it should have been easy to track who had picked me up.

They said they couldn't give out driver information. It sounded like it wasn't policy so much as someone avoiding trouble. Why did I stop there? Why didn't I storm down there? Why didn't I go to the police? I am really angry now that I didn't because if something did happen it would have happened again and again until the little fucker got caught.

I think maybe I didn't go because I didn't have a lot to go on, so I felt like I would be dismissed. Often with these things, it takes a while to process and by that time you have no evidence. Plus, I was hammered at the time so not thinking straight and the next day you wash away any evidence. And, of course, you don't want it to be true.

The other weird thing about the story is that I still had the exact same money on me. I left the club with a tenner for the taxi and still had that ten-pound note on me. So at least he potentially raped me for free!!!

I tried to forgive this taxi driver in my therapy session. A quick hello to Catherine, who is phenomenal and uses a technique called EMDR, which really is fantastic. I've no idea how EMDR works, I never ask, just so long as it does work. How? Well, baby, that's not my business – don't show me the cogs, they're boring – show me the results. I had been able to forgive other similar men using this technique, but for some reason I couldn't forgive this taxi driver. I think it's because he took away my memory. It's hard to forgive if you don't know what you're forgiving, it's hard to accept if you don't know what you're accepting. I try to view it in a more cosmic way, maybe our karmas clashed and I ended up wounded. He's not getting a Christmas card, put it that way.

◆ ◆ ◆

You can become hyper sexualised because you have suffered abuse or trauma or you can just be a physical gal in a physical world in a healthy, balanced way. I would say I have been both in life and now I'm in a very healthy place where I don't use sex to change my state much. In my younger days, like a lot of people, I had very little self-esteem, so I let people use and abuse me. This is not to absolve their part in it. I mean sometimes I was unconscious, so they were definitely to blame.

Nowadays I feel like a different person, so I think it would be harder to enter my space metaphorically and physically if you weren't good for me. Could still happen of course. I mean, there was an incident where a guy tried to rape me in the street. It was just a normal day, I was getting off a bus, and a guy got off at the same stop. He asked me if I knew where a weird-sounding road was. As soon as he asked me, I knew he didn't want directions and my whole body went on high alert. I knew he had a sinister aim. I got out my mobile to phone my mum and started walking. I should have gone into a shop, but that's me thinking with hindsight, and perhaps he would have waited for me anyhow.

It was still light, so I didn't consciously think he would try anything too mad, I just thought I needed to get away from him. So I started to walk home, and explained to my mum about the guy. He then pounced and got his hand in my skirt and tried to get me down on the floor. In the middle of the street. I felt his hand on me, entering my bum (of all the places)! And I screamed, 'Fuck, get the fuck off me' as loud as my lungs would allow. I don't think he was expecting it.

He looked shocked that I was using my voice.

He looked frightened. I looked straight in his eyes and said, 'You never fucking do anything like that again, do you understand me?' I don't know where I found this strength, perhaps because it was daylight on a street and he was unarmed, but I was so angry.

He ran off. Mum was still on the phone, bless her. I felt the imprint of his digit on my 'special entrance' for some time.

I went over to the couple who watched the whole thing and said, 'Do you know what was happening there? He was trying to rape me.' They just nodded. I said, 'Did you think to help me at all?' And the man offered to walk me home. But I was only down the road and I thought he was a pig, so I declined. I reported it to the police, they came round really fast and there was a woman there too, which I was pleased about. I told them that at the end, he looked scared of me and I wondered if it was his first time. They said they very much doubted it and said he probably wasn't that scared. I was just waiting for *one* of them at least to acknowledge I was a double-hard bastard.

Being dysfunctional is not about social standing or class, some of my posh friends are the most fucked up of all. The Tory cabinet anyone????

How to Get a 2.2 from One of the Bottom-ranking Universities

When I was at university, but wait, how did you get to university, you ask? Me, a little messer, who was last seen with an ashtray on her foot, smashing a tray of drinks into a wall? Well, you set your sights as low as possible and then write a popping UCAS form mentioning some of your *made up* hobbies, and none of your *real* ones.

I got accepted into the august establishment of Royal Holloway, which is the 44th best in the UK, don't you know! Other notable alumni (and it is worth noting I didn't qualify for the 99 notable alumni list I pulled this from) include: Emily Davidson, Lenny Henry and a girl I did improv with once who is now a teacher.

I lived in university halls on the Holloway Road and would trot down the stairs to work in the pub below, now called Big Reds. It was an easy life, drinking with people in the pub and doing minimal lectures. I should have been more present and digested the lectures, as I ended up getting 2.2. What in? I hear you cry. Communication and cultural studies. No, I don't know either. Actually a 2.2 isn't bad for someone who when they had the end-of-year ball had taken so many drugs that they were crawling around on the floor, pretty sure they were an Egyptian cat.

I only recently got into learning and quizzing because information is actually pretty cool! The only thing is, I will learn fascinating facts and then forget them immediately. I can play the same quiz game again and again as I will have usually forgotten all the answers. I played a quiz recently on a car journey which my friend had found online and I scored about 65 per cent, which he thought was amazing. He didn't know I'd played exactly the same quiz about five times before.

I honestly think drinking at such a young age damaged my brain somewhat. Did you know that the brain is technically still growing up to the age of twenty-six! What the flip. And I think I wasted a lot of brain-growing time by shrinking it. Well, we're all different I suppose.

I've been sober for over six years now and my memory is getting better and my thinking is clearer, but I do wish I'd never drunk. But then this would be a very different book.

For uni and for a few years after, I hung around with a girl called Amy, she was manic and complex. We used to go clubbing together and she was a great dancer. She tried to teach me but it didn't exactly rub off. Anyhow, Amy was fun and complex and a bit of an addict like me.

When I got sober, the facade and charm of all these friends fell away and we had nothing in common; you change your ways and the social group around you also changes. You love these friends for a time and it's OK that people fade away and are replaced with others; if you change *inside*, your external life changes too, and I find that exciting. Mix it up, swap around, LET SOME OTHERS HAVE A GO!

Amy's mum was a barrister and she used to give us drugs. She'd been supplying Amy's drugs from when she was about fifteen. I couldn't get my head around the fact Amy was from a middle-class family in the system, but still absolutely dysfunctional. But now of course I realise being dysfunctional is not about social standing or class, some of my posh friends are the most fucked up of all. The Tory cabinet anyone????[9]

---

9 NOT my friends, so we are clear.

Once we all went to one of her mum's friends' parties in Cornwall. We drank so much cider and did so many drugs. And yet, once again, I managed to stand out for being in a different world of inebriated. On the way home, Amy's mum had a go at me because I had made it weird. She was disappointed in me. But what do you expect if you give a slightly deranged kid access to unlimited drink and drugs? It's like saying you are disappointed in a monkey for eating all of the bananas – yeah, no shit. How could people get annihilated and act normal and why did I always go overboard and make everyone feel uncomfortable? I was so full of shame, I didn't want to be this way but I didn't know how to be any other way.

One good thing to come out of Cornwall though was that I kissed a guy who looked like Robbie Williams and we decided we were in love. He was as broken as me, just fifteen years older. He came to a house party of mine and my flatmates a few weeks later in London.[10] He drove the whole way on his motorbike, and when he got there I thought, This guy looks nothing like Robbie Williams, and we have no chemistry. I've been had, by drunk me.

He was due to be staying with me all weekend – NIGHTMARE. That was until I got so buckled again

---

10   I know I said I didn't like hosting parties after the fateful one for Craig Prentice, but I lived with five people so I figured between us it would be OK.

that me and my ex (Lion Nose, who I was still madly in love with) locked ourselves in the bathroom and started covering each other with shaving foam and shaving each other's arms. The Robbie Williams tribute act left shortly after that. I did feel bad about that.

Oh and someone had taken a dump in the hallway. Perhaps because he couldn't get into the bathroom with the foam party for two going on.

Shortly after this house party we had to move out. Not turd related, the tenancy was just coming to an end.

The house was around Turnpike Lane – a bit of a grotty area at the time. And not just thanks to me, thank you! I hadn't sorted anywhere else to live and only had a few weeks before turf-out time. But I had other things to do, Primark for one! This was before we had considered the devastating effects of fast fashion, don't you know.

So there I am, walking down the street on my way to Primmy K – a bit chubby, a bit badly dressed, but young enough to carry it off. And this beautiful guy just said hello to me. Not in a letchy way, just with a big open grin; he didn't seem pervy, he seemed vulnerable. If I saw him now, I would probably cotton on to the fact something was a bit off kilter with him. Though at the time I was probably a bit off kilter, too – but to be fair to me, I had very smooth shaved arms.

Anyhow we got talking and swapped numbers. And

I moved in a day or two later. Not because we were desperately in love but because we were looking for something, for someone, to fill the void. And because my tenancy was up.

I distinctly remember unpacking my box of things and laying out some trinkets, thinking, Well, it's nice to set up home – I'M NESTING! This is me now – domestic life has beckoned. Time for me to settle down with my boyfriend.

How batshit crazy is that? I'd known him a few days and we had not really clicked. He would go clubbing with his female best friend until 3 a.m. and I would stay in. I didn't need to go clubbing, I had everything I needed right there. I think it coincided with another sober patch. I think maybe after the house party and the party in Cornwall I just thought, Let's see if life gets better when you quit drinking for a bit. I think this time I lasted about a month. Not ideal but still nice to give the liver a little holiday.

There was a compatibility issue between us, of course. But the bigger issue was, on night one, the very first night... we went to bed, made love, and then he got up, walked into the hallway and slept in the cupboard. Yes, he always slept in the laundry cupboard.

He was a bit embarrassed about it, but there was no budging him. He was like a big, grinning, lovely innocent guy. He was six foot five with a delicate nature, which, mixed with his frame, was absolutely adorable. I moved out after about two weeks. He was really sad but I think just because he didn't like being on his own. The more I think about it, the more I think he might have been on some strong medication, and him sleeping in the cupboard was a symptom of that.

◆ ◆ ◆

By this point I was in the second year of university and I was going to drop out. I applied to be an air steward but I didn't get anywhere and then I had a brain wave: I should run a pub. My mum tried to talk me out of it and I listened a bit but still wanted to do it.

Then Barbie had a word with me. Barbie is my friend's mum who I've known since I was fifteen and she is an absolute grade-A queen. Barbie is as glamorous as she is down-to-earth. She's about seventy-five now, wears pompom slippers, bakes the best cakes and is always giggling and cracking jokes. And she's been married to someone as funny and nice as her for over fifty years. The happiest people I know.

Anyhow, she ever so gently tried to advise me that it would be a bad idea to run a bar and that it is often alcoholics who gravitate towards pub management, so that they can get closer to their poison. I knew what she was saying was true and she managed to steer me away from it and back to my studies. I was lucky because we got student grants when I went to university and rents were manageable. I only really had to work to afford drink and drugs. And 'had to' seems a bit of a stretch.

I remember one of the pretty girls on my course (there were two and predictably they were best friends), anyhow hot girl number one had a very nice jumper on, it was quite unique and looked terrific. I complimented her and asked her where she got it from. She said, 'I got it from Bay Trading, thirty-five pounds.' I remember thinking, I'M NOT SPENDING THIRTY-FIVE POUNDS ON A JUMPER. But I regularly spent that on nights I couldn't remember. More money for bad nights in shit jumpers.

There has to be a better way to feel powerful. Perhaps get very good at rowing boats, crosswords, or strongman competitions?

Do Stolen Bodies Taste Better?

Holloway Road, if you're not familiar with it, is a big ass road in north London. It goes from Archway to Islington and the A1 passes through it (some info for the dads there).

I lived right slap bang in the middle of it for my first year at university and then always hung around its edges. Even now, I'm often cycling or driving up the beast, seeing all the old haunts in my periphery, each time replacing the old memories with better ones.

The road is an eclectic mix of workers' cafes and boujee bistros; it used to house Kiss FM and various high-end erotica shops. There are so many beautiful churches of every different faith. At the top end you have fancy

Islington, where you can get a toaster for £500, and at the other Archway, where you can go to the sexual health clinic for free (big shout-out).

When I was about twenty-five, a couple of years after graduating and moving to Islington, I was walking along the Holloway Road, thinking of some ghosts, and two appeared. Like *Candyman*. It was my old boss Matt from my first pub job and Stanley, an old regular from the pub who I used to be close friends with. It seemed that the old landlord and his regular had kept in touch and remained friends. I hadn't seen either of them for years, so we decided to get on it and catch up.

We pulled a late one, chatting and bustling around the pubs up and down the stretch. It got late, as it sometimes does, and so all three of us went back to Matt's to sleep over. It was pre Uber days.

I woke up to find Stanley and Matt arguing. I figured out quite quickly that Matt was trying to have sex with me while I was out of it. Stanley was shouting at my ex-boss to get off, very much judging him for trying to eff a near corpse.

The thing is, I would have slept with Matt if he'd asked but for him there was no thrill in that. I get it, stolen chips taste better than your own. He wanted to take what wasn't offered, to steal it in my sleep. It doesn't feel nice to wake up to a man trying to take something from you.

I thought Well, at least there's a good guy here, at

least Stanley intervened, and I went back to sleep. Ten minutes later, the 'saviour' Stanley is climbing on top of me trying to insert his dumb little penis, but I woke up and told him to go away. I felt confused and I felt silly. This is how they see me.

Anyway, at least I got the ex-boss back by pissing in his bed. Actually, he was staying at his mum's house, so yet again the woman ultimately suffers lol. The next day I felt bad about the bed and what he would think of me. I was the one who felt shame about getting so drunk. I had so little self-esteem, I wasn't even initially angry about what the guys did, I just felt so embarrassed about getting so drunk that they could do that.

◆ ◆ ◆

One producer has date-raped so many women using drugs – yeah, so not all drugs are kewl – and he honestly doesn't seem to think he's done anything wrong. A friend told me she was raped by him, and another woman refused to work with him because he had raped her. She needed the money but turned down an amazing job because he was the producer and she couldn't face seeing him. Then came a write-up in *The Guardian*, where lots of people had come forward with their stories. He's drugged and raped so many women and he's still posting boomerang videos on Instagram stories about being at Soho House. Absolutely infuriating.

Although, hilariously, with this rapey producer, I was at his house off my box once and he never touched me – the one person he didn't want to date-rape!

Only one in a hundred rapes recorded by police in 2021 resulted in a charge the same year – that's a charge, not a conviction. The conviction rates are even more depressing.

There has to be a better way to feel powerful. Perhaps get very good at rowing boats, crosswords, or strongman competitions? Just some ideas there if any rapists are reading along.

A funny story (finally): I had initially spoken about other people's stories here too and this section was a lot longer and a friend (top comic and mid-level cutie pie John Robins) was reading it back and hadn't laughed for a while and I said, 'Oh no, you haven't laughed for ten minutes' and he said, 'Well, I am on my fourth rape story, m'love,' and then we really laughed and I made some edits to keep things a tad lighter. 'What, this is the light version?' I hear you cry! Yep, hope you're enjoying it!

Do we need these stories in an autobiography about a comic and snail impersonator, I hear you yelp? And that's a terrific question, Steven, but I wanted to talk about all the dark and shade. I didn't want to leave it out, as it is part of life. Plus, this book is about overcoming darkness and shame, and so to deny the bits of life that cause darkness and shame would be remiss.

Honest discussion is an antidote to shame, and it's the only way to garner change.

One of the wisest, simplest things I've ever read about sex comes from *Alcoholics Anonymous* aka 'The Big Book' and it goes like this:

'Our sex powers were God-given, and therefore good, neither to be used lightly or selfishly, nor to be despised nor loathed.'

How many problems would be solved if that was the mantra we all lived by when it came to sex? All the religions in the world screwed us up so much with fear and shame and violence when it comes to sex, and it took a couple of old drunks to get to the truth. But you can tell something majestic had a hand in it – after all, it's on page 69 (true story).

Always try and bring them off too, for equality.

Not Every Massage is a Couples' Massage

None of this stopped me being a little slut. I did **EXACTLY WHAT I WANTED (Alexa, play Beyoncé).** And then suffered great shame afterwards (Alexa, stop Beyoncé).

I THINK I've stopped using sex as a tool for my emotions. What I crave now is a deep connection with one person. But of course I have been at times just a horny girl in a horny world. Although, like I say, in my later years, not in a damaged way. More like a sassy business lady making sure the deal works for everyone. On that note…

How on earth are people having massages and not wanting to be brought off?! How? You are naked under a towel and a stranger is touching you in a way that says, 'I know we just met, but I want you to bear my many children.'

I don't have one-night stands any more – because my boyfriend doesn't like it. Lol. Nah, I've always been a very physical person and, as you may have picked up on by now, I love excitement, so I've had some interesting escapades. There's been some stuff I wouldn't do now, but it's all very useful in learning how to set boundaries and respect yourself and see what feels good emotionally and physically for you and the other person. I think many women enjoy being physical as much as some men, but we're told that we should save our tuppences for a special occasion. Ludicrous. THEY MIGHT GO OFF!!!!

I've had a few happy endings in massages in the past and I cannot work out how I feel about it. Safe to say I'm no longer booking massages.

My first was in Lanzarote (but the nice side) with a beautiful Brazilian guy. He said not to wear any bikini, so that's asking for trouble. The hour massage lasted two hours (the last hour was EXTRA, if you catch my drift). He just kept going near my erogenous areas, if you know what I mean (my undercarriage) and it just built up, until it was impossible not to direct his hand to exactly where I wanted it. This sounds pretty risky but he'd already brushed past me with a massive boner and we had already gone overtime. He could of course have taken his hand away, but he was pretty game immediately.

We didn't sleep together but messed about. He wanted my room number, but I had to say no as I was on a mini break with another guy I had just started seeing. But don't worry, we had split up on the flight over. We realised quickly that we were incompatible; me when he told me his favourite song was Robbie Williams' 'Angels'! And him when he saw me eating! So we were just going as friends with benefits but it seemed a bit uncouth to wheel in a third member.

A fun fact about this guy I was dating for a week: he presented me with a professional personality test – commissioned by his business (they are usually used to measure employee suitability) – and I was narcissistic enough to complete it. What I didn't realise was that he was using it to work out if I was wife material. Reader, I was not.

Anyway back to the massage story... People ask me how you get from a professional massage to, well, a non-professional massage. And it's very easy – you just make the right noises! All the thrill of it is in the subtle growing of sexual energy between you both. You have to make sure they're into it though, otherwise you're no better than a sleazy guy at the Christmas party. It's about nuance; it's about patience. If they are on the same page, it builds slowly, a few noises, lingering hands on certain areas, a few questions like 'Is there anything you don't like?' and you answer with

'Do anything.' They might rub their leg against your hand, you let out a sigh… and the kundalini unravels. That's the exciting bit, seeing if you are both feeding this beast of physical potential.

Once, in London, a masseuse stopped the massage, we fooled around for a bit and both came, and then the guy said I had fifteen minutes left of the massage, so he diligently went back to kneading my big calf muscles. What a guy!

I don't think it's ideal that I did it to be fair. I have had a few and usually feel weird afterwards, so that's it for me. It was nice while it lasted. It's almost like you are giving into an energy that controls you, and I think it's better to control it. To go 'higher', as my old healer used to say. That's what I said to the masseuse – ooorr errr etc., etc.

If a man did this we would think he was a bit gross. But then it's to do with the balance and history of power. Also, in my defence, I would always try and bring them off too, for equality, so that I wasn't like a Roman emperor throwing money at servants to jazz me off.

Only once did the guy refuse to come himself. He thought it was unprofessional if he came, too. He said, 'It wouldn't feel right but I would love to touch you, if you don't mind. It's a great stress reliever!'

I should have guessed from his name: Alan. Lovely, kind Alan. Could have also guessed from his sandals.

Very Alan. To be fair to his footwear, I'm surprised he jazzed me off at all.

I guess I liked doing it because it was a transaction with no emotional buy-in, a mechanical exchange, if you will. Everyone was happy, and everyone knew where they stood; we wouldn't pretend we wanted to see each other again. I wasn't ready for a relationship so this seemed like a way of having some of a relationship (the part where you jack each other off) but not *any* of the rest. And there were benefits to that, but I still felt odd after. There was a vulnerable feeling that I had shared too much or let a horny feeling drive me in the heat of the moment. Is that society's guilt, parental guilt or just that there probably were better things I could be doing with my time than letting a stranger into my house and body?

Well, no shame now, it's done and it was ultimately 62 per cent fun. The thing is you can wazz yourself off with no weirdness whatsoever: it's quicker, safer and free. And I do it in my sandals, so you never have to lose the sandals. Make it your own, guys, put up some bunting, dress as an Elizabethan, just have fun with it!

If one person is bobbing the head, so should another, as the old saying goes. To doff a cap, as it were – I'm talking about cunnilingus ;).

The Worst Drug Dealer of All Time

I was an ambitious woman, even alongside my degree I found the time to do a night class in how to be a drug dealer. There was a guy who came into the pub I worked in who was a bit dodgy; he dealt drugs, he'd been to prison and wasn't my type at all, so obviously I slept with him. Luckily, the sex was terrible. I don't think you can blame one person for bad sex because it's just chemistry or nerves. Unless – as was the case with this twit – they are a selfish Simon! If one person is bobbing the head, so should another, as the old saying goes. To doff a cap, as it were – I'm talking about cunnilingus ;).

The only thing worse than being lazy and mean-spirited in bed is then arrogantly bigging yourself up afterwards. He was like 'Oh you loved that, didn't you... If you thought that was good, next time will be even better.' Then he told me what he benched. ARE YOU HIGH OR DUMB OR BOTH? He was his own stupid hype man. When I say he bigged himself up *after*, he also bigged himself up *during* the act too.

If that happened these days I would look him squarely in the peepers and say, 'Well Mr hoggish, that experience was bleak and lacklustre and you have the manners of a slug. And if you do not offer to go down on a lady then they will leave bitterly disappointed by your selfish below-mediocre sex. Now good day to you.'

But what I did instead was buy loads of cocaine from him to sell on. I used my student loan to assist me in a canny bulk-buy manoeuvre. He convinced me to do it because he had some great stuff but he wanted to go straight, but *I* could earn some money. Get some nose up and then sell it on to students and I thought, Well, he owes me this. What a super idea.

Walking down the Holloway Road with a load of drugs on me, I felt kind of bad but kind of cool IF ANYONE KNEW?! I could get arrested! Well, I wouldn't have far to travel if I did; I could see Holloway's notorious prison for ladies from my bedroom window.

I got back to my uni room and secreted the drugs. I guess now I'd just wait and see who wants to be linked up. I wouldn't be a street seller, I'd wait till people came to me in the pub or wherever, that way I wasn't the bad guy, they were doing it anyhow. I didn't feel too grotty about it, because I did it myself all the time anyhow. And I'd make a bit of money too. I started crunching all the numbers in my head.

That night I sauntered into the pub with my new persona – yeah, I walked a bit differently now. I understood *Reservoir Dogs* in a deeper way, I was a bit more of a gal to know. I slinked in and did a shift behind the bar – even though I was a big-time dealer now, I was still loyal to the old crew.

I was sitting on this new info about me in the way that a kid sits on a ten-pound note; it's not going to be long before everyone knows about it. I casually drop it into the conversation with my boss, Matt, that I have a stash of cocaine and we agree we should all do some.

So him, me and Jo do some. Jo was a firecracker of a girl. She was a blonde, short, pretty Irish girl who would think nothing of booting a load of drunk men out of the pub. And people just did what she said. She was a great force to be reckoned with for many reasons, *and* she was the only staff member who didn't want to sleep with Matt.

We all do some coke, pouring ourselves drinks, waiting to come up. Nothing. We just sit there as my heart sinks into a pool of embarrassment. I've been mugged off. Mortifying.

And just like that, my drug-dealing career ended. At the time I was so ashamed I'd been ripped off, but now I am so grateful, I don't think dealing coke is great karma. There have been a few near misses like that, often great news is dressed up as bad news.

A week later, Matt slung the guy who ripped me off out of the pub and I was really pleased. What a dick, coming back into the pub after that. Matt chucked him out, saying, 'That's for selling my staff shit coke.' I was so delighted he stuck up for me. It was as near to a tribe as I had. Tragic that I was pleased with that, he didn't even say 'friend', he said 'staff'. He owned me, I worked for him. None of it was about loyalty to me of course; it was just men pissing over their corner of the street. And only but four years later, I would urinate in his mother's spare room. Isn't life strange?!

Not all pigs are swines.

The Altar of Gibraltar

After nine months of intense study (six hours a week), I decided to go to Gibraltar for the summer because someone told me that on this island, it was a couple of quid for a bottle of vodka.

The guy who told me that was a manager at the pub. I didn't know this but he was stealing from the tills and doing this big showdown every night to see whose till was short, and which one of the girls was stealing. He would keep us all there in suspense and suspicion while he counted the tills. We all felt so scared and so upset that someone had been stealing. It was horrible. He told me years later it WAS HIM. And everyone in pubs does it. I could not believe it. I was pretty naive. Anyhow, I guess these days there's cameras.

Still, he had got me work in Gibraltar and a place to stay at his sister's for a good price, and she was really nice.

So off I went to my Mecca (Gibraltar), in search of my God (booze).

Gibraltar was hot all the time, you could walk to most places, and if you were lucky you might see some small monkeys. There wasn't a unifying feel to the place, it was predominantly English pubs doing fry-ups, with the occasional smattering of Spanish culture (omelettes). I met a lot of tattooed expats with names like Dave and Mike.

It was a weird place, the locals didn't seem to enjoy humour, or maybe it was just our humour. A lot of them were very straight down the line. We would make jokes with punters in the bar and they would answer us back very seriously. It was a strange old vibe; being a small island, everyone appeared to know each other, and their values seemed to be from another time. A lot of the girls were keen to get married super-early, maybe there's not a lot else to do there. At the time, there didn't seem to be a lot of culture, but then maybe it was me and I wasn't looking for it. It's fun for a week or two, but living there for eight weeks got a bit 'Groundhog Day'. The repetitiveness of it would have turned me into an alcoholic if I wasn't one already.

Gibraltarians tend to speak English and Spanish and

with their English, they often have their own intonations, so it's sometimes a little funny to hear because it has its own rhythm.

You could cross the border into Spain, by just walking across the road with your passport; a man in a hut would check it and then suddenly you were in another country. People didn't bother popping into Spain that often.

The place I got a job was an upmarket bistro on the waterfront, called Bianca's. I say 'upmarket', it was upmarket for Gibraltar. It was right on the quayside and sold club sandwiches and salmon and potatoes. I think it would have been *more* upmarket if I wasn't working there.

It was in a beautiful setting and people would sit outside watching the sea with a crisp white wine. And sometimes a wine with lemonade in – oookay babe. The manager was a little white guy called Len who always wore chino shorts and was largely fine. There were a lot of friendly Moroccan chefs in the kitchen, and they were lovely, apart from when they would monitor my chip intake, because they said I was getting fat. I just told them to piss off. They weren't wrong though.

They all wore a pair of Moroccan slippers and changed in the kitchen. One day my friend found me face down in the Moroccan slippers, too hungover to get up.

I made good friends with a girl a few years older than me called Mish. She looked like a model – well, she was a model, but she'd left the business in part because she didn't like it, and in part because she needed to go undercover. She had changed her name and had run away to Gibraltar because her ex-boyfriend was very controlling and tried to destroy her when she plucked up the courage to leave. He was actively trying to hunt her down, so she had to move away from all of her family and friends to another country.

On the upside, Mish would get loads of tips because she was so fit (and sure, good at her job). She threw herself into her new life, and didn't let things hold her back for long. She would get A LOT of offers too. Quite often from a guy who was on a date with his wife or girlfriend at the time, and they would proposition Mish while their partner was in the toilet or smoking outside.

After a while she resented these creeps, and she started to tell the women what their fella had said to her, in front of him. On those occasions it's fair to say she usually got less of a tip. Pretty amusing to out the cheeky swines though; yes, she was getting her spirit back.

The Bianca's uniform was a red shapeless polo shirt teamed up with some big, stocky navy shorts – think boy scouts, think no thank you! The shorts were bunched up and big at the hips and three-quarter length, so the shape really accentuated my weird knees and big hips. They suited no one, well, apart from Mish.

I also made great friends with Gee. She was also an

absolute babe, a beautiful creature with very blonde hair and the biggest, bluest eyes. She looked like an angel – a beautiful angel with a mouth like a sewer. Gee and I were best friends for the summer, perhaps because she had a great dry sense of humour, we were both single, and we both loved caning it.

One night, Gee and I went to the local nightclub and the themed night was 'beach babes' or something: a thinly veiled excuse to get all the chicks to wear bikini tops. Gee and I thought it was a load of sexist nonsense, but we were still going to go.

We finished our shift and went to the garage to get a bottle of whisky to drink at the roundabout. We went for a bottle of Four Roses because it was so very cheap and for some reason the name made us laugh, perhaps the elegance of the name against the cheapness and the hardness of it. We sat on the grassy roundabout and swigged our Four Roses, chatting freely as the warm nectar slid down our little throats.

Then we got changed.

We thought it would be funny to play a different game and wear full beachwear to the club. Imagine: big Bermuda shorts, snorkels, and bright sun cream over our faces. One of us wore big flippers, and one of us popped on a big floppy sun hat. We turned up to the club really laughing at our own joke 'BEACH BABES'. Predictably it was full of girls who had adhered to the memo and were wearing sexy bikinis, hot pants and sarongs. The doorman looked at us, put his hand over his mouth, sort of gasped in horror and seemed really sad for us.

Doorman: 'What are you doing?'

Us: 'We thought it was beach themed?'

Doorman: 'Oh no, no, no girls, not like that.'

Us: 'Oh how embarrassing.'

Doorman: 'Yes (pitifully), well you can come in anyhow, OK, girls (ushering us quickly). Maybe take off what you can.'

We thought we were so funny and, let me tell you, no one else seemed to enjoy it as much as us. But if someone doesn't enjoy your comedy, it's important to double down.

Later that night the police tried to arrest me for being drunk and disorderly – but I was trying to tell them that I was just being a bit of a laugh. They were quite jovial about it, but I really could not be doing with going to a police cell and I think someone mentioned a fine too. They said if I could walk in a straight line they would let me off. I was quite drunk but I really focused and I absolutely smashed it, and then started dancing triumphantly and even though I was being annoying with my victory dance, they stuck to their word of not arresting me #notallpigsareswines.

Always trust a man with indoor and outdoor slippers.

Beating the Rugby Team

(Crucially Not at Rugby)

After my European summer, I was back, slap bang in the middle of the Holloway Road, telling everyone what a *tinto de verano* was.

I was coming back to the second year of uni a little bit wiser, I'd lived in another country for goodness' sake: I'd learnt five words in Spanish, I'd met a *man* called Michelle, I'd been scuba diving in a swimming pool. Nothing could hold me back. I decided to let my talents shine and I entered a local drinking competition. It was at a pub I used to drink in by Holloway Tube. The advert said there was a first and second place prize and the winner got to choose from a four-day holiday to Spain or a big TV.

I went into training and took it seriously. I crammed, I practised and I visualised winning.

Come the night, I was calm and confident. I went in focused and ready to tip this brown liquid down my gullet and not stop until I had emptied the vessel. There weren't many women in the fight, so the crowd were largely on my side. Except for the rugby team, who really wanted to win and who did not cheer me on at all. But I did win by quite a lovely margin – sorry boyz.

I opted for the TV, but I actually asked the landlord which was worth more and he made a face as if to say, 'Well, I don't think that's very classy.' And I thought quite right too and picked the telly. I didn't have one at the time, so it was ideal. And I'd just bloody been to Spain.

I'd never won anything before. Maybe I had found my purpose in life! 'I'd like to thank God, my sponsors and my gag reflexes!'

I was going out with this handsome guy at the time who was the year above me at university, he was called Pete. He must have only been twenty-one but he had life sorted – a Volkswagen Golf, on the way to a stable management job and two pairs of slippers (indoor and outdoor). Maybe I was too young to appreciate it then, but now I would say: always trust a man with indoor and outdoor slippers.

I met him while I was working on a pub shift. He came in and I thought, That's my type: long brown hair, kind, strong face and a lovely line in chat. Northern too. Sign me up. He'd drop in regularly but I didn't have that obsessive thing around him, I liked him but I wouldn't self-destruct if he didn't flirt with me. Maybe because he was safe, so couldn't detonate me. At this stage we were just flirting and I noticed he hadn't been in for a bit, so when he came back we had a chat that went like this:

Me: 'Where have you been?'

Pete: 'Well, funny story actually, I had to go to the hospital, quite suddenly.'

Me: (Being silly) 'Ooo – did you snap your banjo string?'

Pete: 'WHAT – HOW DID YOU GUESS THAT?'

If you don't know what a banjo string is, here's the dictionary definition: 'the small tag of skin on the underside of your penis, between your foreskin and the shaft of your penis'. Enjoy your new-found knowledge.

It was a total fluke, I was guessing, but maybe he glanced down at his bits as he was speaking.

Or, maybe I am a bit mystical. My mum maintains we are descended from traveller stock, so that would explain a lot.

But that's how we met and went out for a year and a half. We bonded over the banjo. A STORY AS OLD AS TIME. And yes, I did have to be ever so careful with it the first time we messed about.

So the night I beat the rugby team in the back of the

pub, I was ecstatic, my first taste of fame. No one could believe this chick beat all these burly men. My favourite kind of victory – subverting stereotypes. And getting a new TV for it.

Pete carried me out on his shoulders, proud as punch. We both were. He liked my rebellious side. I would often drink beer in the mornings when I was with him, but I was playing a character, I didn't really have a problem. It was just funny, I was a student and it was cool, they did it in music videos. I didn't *need* it. When I finally got around to finishing with lovely, beautiful Pete, I said it was because I knew I had a bit of a drink problem and that I was going to address it. He said he would help me and we could stay together, I reiterated that I needed to do it on my own. But really I had no intention of sorting it out. I wanted to be wild and free and self-destructive and he was too sorted for me.

One thing I cannot stand is nepotism, unless I am benefitting from it.

An Apology to Andi Peters

I finished university bloated and with very thin eyebrows – I didn't keep in touch with anyone I'd met there, I hadn't really found my people.

The main thing is I needed a job. I wanted to work in TV and I had sent hundreds of speculative letters and official applications but I didn't get one interview. I don't think it was anything personal – they hadn't seen the eyebrows – but it's a competitive industry, everyone wants a job where you have to gunk a presenter or what not. I mean, I guess another issue might have been I had no idea what happens in TV.

While I was waiting for a TV company to employ me, I worked in an architects' firm in Putney. The lady gave me the job because the way I had my hair reminded her of

Rogue from *X-Men*. I couldn't file for shit but I was fun to have around and I really did try. In my defence the filing system in an architects' office is pretty complicated. I wasn't going to get my head around that in a year. Do superheroes file?

Every day I had a whole family-size baguette with a bowl of soup for lunch. A whole big baguette. Sorry, has anyone seen the rest of my baguette because I will be eating the entire French stick with my bowl of soup?

After a year and a half I managed to get a work-experience role on *SM:TV CD:UK*, which was a really popular show at the time. Ant and Dec had just moved on and Tess Daly and James Redmond had taken the reins. One thing I cannot stand is nepotism, unless I am benefiting from it. And my boyfriend at the time got me the job through his friend. I was paid a minimal amount, but I had some savings to live off for a bit and then worked some shifts in a pub too as the work was only on the weekends. My boyfriend was called Mark and he worked in music. I felt quite insecure in the relationship because he had written books and was about to interview Madonna and I had done nothing with my life.

These days, having had some external success, I know that in romantic relationships most people just crave connection, not status. But I didn't know that then, I just wanted to be 'someone'.

AN APOLOGY TO ANDI PETERS

Here's a list of jobs I did before and during comedy:

- For two weeks I was a runner on a show with Andi Peters. One day I hadn't made him enough tea and I saw him pull a face about me to someone else when he had to *ask* me for a tea. I was mortified, I hadn't realised. I wish he'd just told me though rather than making faces about me, but I got my own back on him recently because I was at some TV studios and needed the toilet quite badly. The security let me through to an area where his dressing room happened to be (unlocked), so I took a massive shit in there (in the toilet tbf) and used his cologne. He's probably a very nice man and I was probably a very bad runner, so sorry, Andi!

- I worked in TV in development for the BBC. I kept pitching things with cats in and they had to say, 'Look, we're looking for the next Apprentice, not the next Cats in Hats.' Understood... Have you seen my latest treatment for Cats *Not* in Hats?

- My friend had a food van she took to festivals and me and one of my best friends, Georgie, worked on it. This was fun work and she could never sack us, even though we drunk loads and ate all the flakes. Hard to sack us when we largely got paid in food and good times.

- After university I had a telesales job selling CDs on

the phone – they were naff collections about thirty CDs long to rinse the money from people. They had titles like *County and Western for You Right Now*. It was mainly young people who worked at the call centre, and we would dare each other to get random sentences into the conversations with customers. Great fun until one guy got the sack for pushing his luck and saying, 'And just how big are your breasts, madam?' That was bad enough but every time she asked him to repeat himself, he would say it louder and clearer, until she said she was recording him and would be taking legal action.

- I worked for a healthcare company on reception and we could wear our own clothes. But shortly after I joined they enforced a uniform, because my interpretation of smart casual was too loose. I felt awful I had ruined the run for everyone.

- I worked at Ofcom as a PA and my bosses were lovely. I was bang average. A year after I left (of my own accord for once), they had to handle a complaint about me and the board there made a ruling that I was not allowed on Absolute Radio live for a whole year. Maybe they missed me and were trying to bar me from showbizzzniss so I had to come back to them – nice try, Ofcom! Nice try!

AN APOLOGY TO ANDI PETERS

I was mortified about the Absolute Radio situation. My friend Geoff Lloyd had been kind enough to give me a chance filling in for a show or two and co-hosting with him. Geoff is such a funny, delightful, generous man, and he's one of the best broadcasters out there, so to co-host with him on a show was a gift, a gift I should have taken better care of.

The producer of the show was a nice woman called Amy. I had worked with her on an internet radio show, where you can just say anything, so I was in that mindset. I don't remember anyone telling me to watch my language, I guess because I am a grown woman and it's really obvious not to be rude on National Radio at 6 p.m.

I've since done lots of live TV and radio and would never ever make that mistake again. However, on this occasion with me being green and silly, Geoff asked me for a chat-up line and it played out a bit like this:

Geoff: 'You've got some chat-up lines, haven't you Lou?'

Lou: 'Yes, let's do a role play. Excuse me, do you have the time…?'

Geoff: 'It's…'

Lou: 'To suck me off?!'

Geoff: 'Oh dear, I'm very sorry to anyone who was offended by that, let's go to a song. This is "Shouldn't Do That" by Kajagoogoo.'

I felt terrible. There were only a few complaints but Ofcom had to investigate them. One woman emailed in to say: 'I had to explain what suck me off meant to my eight-year-old kid.' Erm. Did you?

I felt so bad for the people working at the radio station and for Geoff. That was a headache they did not need.

◆ ◆ ◆

In my early twenties, I worked as an assistant (glorified runner) for a big film company in London. My friend got me the job and I was drafted in every few months when they were overloaded. I would be stuffing envelopes, which sounds boring until you consider I was sending them to people like Helena Bonham Carter and Emma Thompson.

And then a month later, I would go to the actual premiere! Very exciting. The first time I went to a premiere I could not believe my eyes, the amount of money they must have spent on attaching a car to the ceiling for one film, or recreating a gigantic imagined French brothel for another – it was mesmerising, exciting and a little bit 'ooo look at the disparity of wealth, all this for one night for famous people' but, hey, that's the world we live in and it's not like I didn't enjoy the free canapés and cocktails. I'm not sure they go to such lengths now, so I was lucky to witness it.

Back in the office, I stuck out like a broken thumb. My friend had got the job because her stepbrother was very high up in the LA office and I'd got the job because I knew her and they needed someone who someone could vouch for. In that world it's usually a friend, or a friend of a friend, who walks through the door. You don't want someone off the streets in case they are secretly scribbling down Helena Bonham Carter's address. Which I have included in the notes section.

I was in the PR department and everyone seemed to be very similar, even their names: Tilly, Milly, Frilly. PR women are often a certain breed. Of course I know some who are a right laugh but generally it attracts a distinct personality type. OR does the *industry* create carbon copies once they are in the job? I saw one younger girl coming through and she looked like the rest of them in that office: thin, blonde, and like she knew her way around a stable, but she was different – she didn't have a rehearsed way of speaking, she didn't say everything as if she was being filmed for a behind-the-scenes piece at *Vanity Fair*, and she didn't act as if her job of putting Tom Hanks in a car was a game-changing moment for humanity. She was more natural when she spoke, she laughed easily, took a genuine interest in people and seemed comfortable in her own skin. I worked with her for a week and really warmed to her.

I came back six months later and she was dressed

head to toe in black, she was speaking in an affected manner, and had developed a robotic coldness. What a fascinating ride!

Anyhow, they might have been right to treat me with trepidation as I did eventually mess up in a way that Milly, Tilly and Frilly would not have. At a big premiere I was supposed to be looking after a producer, but I was embarrassed to just hang around his table in case he needed anything, I mean, food and drinks were being brought round to the tables – what did he need me for, my recent thoughts on the Syrian war? No, this was humiliating for both of us, so I took myself off to enjoy the cocktails. I basically left him to it all night and got drunk. Apparently he was looking for his car at the end of the night and one of the women said Lou is supposed to sort that and another concurred that I was in no fit state for that role: last seen speaking to Clive Owen with so much cocktail down my shirt the whole thing had gone a completely different colour. From white to pink.

That night I stayed in The Dorchester – my friend had hooked up with someone in the company who was staying there and I slept in the bath.

They stopped using me quite soon after this. I did go to one more party though just because my friend had a plus-one so I bummed along. And this time, it was my turn to pull a big company suit. The guy I pulled was really fit and really easy to talk to. When I bumped into him, he was going to go and had a car booked to take him back to Hertfordshire or wherever he lived, but when he saw me he must have thought, here's a girl I can get smashed with. Absolutely spot on, mate. We got more drinks, went out for a smoke and he said he could get us a hotel on his company card.

We rampaged round the streets of Soho looking for the best hotel that had availability. We were turning up at some pretty nice places, one of which turned us away because I tried to eat one of the display apples. It was made of glass.

Eventually we found a very nice establishment. I was telling reception we wanted the honeymoon suite, for a laugh, but I guess that's quite hard to get through on expenses. The guy found it funny but opted for a double instead and it was by far the fanciest hotel I had ever stayed in (if you don't include sleeping in the bath at The Dorchester).

He was great company and we stayed up talking and kissing. I actually liked him a lot, which is a shame as I pissed in the bed and tried to blame it on him. He didn't ask for my number, but at least I had something to blame it on! If only I hadn't wet the bed, we would be married by now. I hope he was OK to put the extra mattress-cleaning charge on the company account.

I was actually mortified because obviously I wanted the handsome, successful man to fall in love with me, but instead he would be waking up with regret and texting his friends to say he pulled a weirdo, while I had to rush straight into work at my crappy job in the same crappy clothes. Luckily, they were urine-free though, as I wet the bed in my birthday suit.

By this time I had a receptionist's job in a TV company. When I got to work, I figured out the format of his work email and sent him an apology. No bounce back. But crucially no reply either. Mortifying.

Men are people too!

Poppadoms Don't Preach

I didn't trust men and didn't treat them that nicely because I honestly didn't think they were real people with real emotions. I remember my mum saying to me, 'You do know that men have emotions, don't you?' And I thought, Yeah, but not REALLY. I just assumed that all #men were at best self-centred liars, and at worst, rapists. SORRY FELLAS.

The data I had collected from a small sample group did sometimes skew/screw that way. But now I've met better, so I know better. It turns out, men are people too! No more lady-incel vibes here.

Anyhow, my heart was behind a locked fence, so I went out with people but I was a bit of a taker and couldn't really give myself emotionally.

After the wet-bed debacle, I did end up with someone for a couple of years. He was the guy who interviewed Madonna and he was lovely. I met him on a snowboarding holiday and he seemed exciting AND nice. But after two years, I split up with him, very suddenly over one small white lie.

I finished it abruptly because he told me he hadn't been to a strip club on a stag do. However, I had seen a paper receipt in his room, so I knew he had. He said he lied because he knew I hated them. After that one lie, he was dead to me. I finished the two-year relationship in an Indian restaurant. Mid-poppadom.

In fairness, he shouldn't have lied, but finishing it so abruptly after two years was extreme. He was so shocked and so upset. He begged me to see his point of view but I had gone into a cold place where I just watched him like a stranger, thinking, fuck you. Any lies made me shut down and run away.

He left the restaurant crying and I ate my meal, then his, and never contacted him again.[11] That must have been so painful for him after two years of sharing our lives together; I think he called my mum and hung up because he didn't know what else to do. But I was numb because I'd never really fully let him in. You can't get as hurt if you don't let them in, but you don't get to fully

---

11   Except to apologise about ten years later.

experience the relationship either. And you can cause a lot of damage.

I apologised years later for not treating him better and he said, 'That's OK – it prepared me for a string of heartless nutters.' Oh dear, I guess he had a type. Although he must have grown out of it, because I think he's in a happy relationship now. And he's interviewed Madonna, so… he's thriving.

What's good for the goose isn't necessarily good for the gander. For example, my friend likes his balls stretched and scratched, and I, for example, don't have balls.

Fake It Till You Break It

By this point, I had a job as a receptionist at a TV company and whilst I was outwardly extrovert, I would cry if someone said, 'Well done.' I wondered why I had the attitude of a humble servant and my head hung like a naughty donkey.

It took me years to unpick it. I could do fake confidence, I'd learnt that in spades. I once had an interview to be a researcher in TV and was so confident in the interview, I really knew how to sell myself and my ideas. But when it came to the actual job, I was so embarrassed at every turn. Low self-esteem, threatened by the rich, clever girl I worked with (her dad bought her a flat in Covent Garden for crying out loud AND loved her AND she was so smart)?!

I was so paranoid they'd sack me, I actually went looking for emails about me. It turns out they *were* planning to sack me. If I'd been confident in what I brought and focused on what I WAS rather than what I WASN'T, then that experience could have been wildly different. I had a pattern though: I would get a job and then spiral, *knowing* that I wasn't good enough, which then became a self-fulfilling prophecy, and I would berate and hate myself until everyone else did.

I do have self-esteem and self-belief now and I am calmer in my body. And that's only taken about fifteen years of throwing absolutely everything at it because of the pain caused by not having it. Of course I am privileged, although I did start the journey when I was skint and there is lots of free stuff you can do: meditations on YouTube, tapping videos, breathing, repeating affirmations, reading library books or free PDFs online, etc. But it's not an equal world. I try to pay back and have bought tons of cranial appointments for lots of skint or unwilling (ha) friends, some relatives and sometimes even a chef or an ex. I mean is it a good turn if they have no interest in going?! No, it's a waste of money and time, but I'd do it all again. Sarrrry!

I should explain cranial sacral therapy as I am always banging on about it. Cranial sacral is a division of osteopathy, so they study for years, thank you! And it is a legit practice, no matter what your uncle says. The NHS even recommends it as one of the only things that helps babies with colic. So if you're reading this and you're a little baby with colic, why wait any longer?! The practitioners are often also extremely intuitive and they seem to be working on the mind, body and soul as one. It's been epic for me but, and this is a big caveat I suppose: it doesn't work for everyone.

Once I was in LA and I booked a cranial appointment and when I turned up he said, 'Where's the injury?'

I said, 'Oh no, it's just for emotional stuff.' He looked at me blankly. I tried to explain: 'Back home, they sort of tap into your energy field.'

He looked a bit cross if anything. 'Right. Well, I'm strictly injury based.'

And we both left it as a learning experience. Shame I had driven an hour to get there. Shame he didn't get paid. Nice guy to chalk it down to a misunderstanding. Maybe he's more spiritual than he thinks ;)

My friend's mum went to a cranial sacral therapist and it released something in her and she cried for three days. We thought that was great, it must have shifted something! But she thought, 'Why would I pay good money to cry for three days?', which I do understand. And what's good for the goose isn't necessarily good for the gander. For example, my friend likes his balls stretched and scratched, and I, for example, don't have balls.

It's true everyone struggles in their twenties to a greater or lesser extent, we're all trying to figure out who we are – a luxury of the free world, I suppose. But some people just seem to have it together. My friend Sally was so capable – she was organising whole TV shoots while I was on reception, crying because somebody complimented my pencil. I didn't know who I was and I was so paranoid with friends, too. I remember Sally was reading a book once and I said: 'I don't read enough, I don't think I've got a soul' and burst into tears – which really makes us laugh now. And here I am WRITING a book – wonder if I'll read this one?! Spoiler: no, I got Sally to read it for me. What's funny is I genuinely did get her to read the first version and the bitch gave me some great notes. I just called her a bitch to see if she reads this version.

Although I could scrape by, never once did I think I had anything worth offering the world. There must be so many people like this and I wish I could scoop them up and tell them that they do, I wish everybody knew that everyone has something to offer the world.

Maybe that's what happens when someone loses their power over you: they look shorter.

Some Deep Detective Work in Chiswick

After my reception job in the TV company with the lovely Sally, I moved jobs and worked for a corporate TV production company in West London. **It was way more money and responsibility but the output was DULL.** Health and safety videos and other bone-dry affairs.

The boss had a 4 x 4 and owed loads of people money. So many people own Land Rovers in Chiswick, it's as if the M4 is farmland. He was an absolute tool, so naturally I fancied him. He was another middle-aged man who wanted to 'collect the set'. And by that I mean sleep with all his female employees, and he managed it, so a real goal setter! Although the company was quite small – just the three chicks under him if you'll excuse the pun. He didn't like me much. It was just a one-night thing, and he liked me less when I broke his bed, and not in a sexy way. Standing up after the event, as opposed to any great during-action.

One night after work, we all went clubbing in Chiswick, which sounds like an oxymoron but there we go – there is a club in Chiswick and I was in it.

At one point I was dancing on the stage because I put the SHOW into show pony (or the HO). And this guy comes over and shrugs at me like I know him, so I think Well, I must know him and I hazard a guess: 'Anze?'

Anze was a guy I was seeing at university (for about ten days). And he nods, yeah it's Anze. I could not believe it was Anze after all these years. I knew I would bump into him again.

My biggest memory of him at uni was him looking broad and lean and beautiful as we went to get some food at two in the morning and a group of girls in the place clearly fancied him. He came back over to my table, showing off for them, singing but gesticulating at me. He sung this song which still sticks in my head: 'Nice and lovely, that's how she loves me.' I was hooked.

He lived with his mum in a big house near Holloway Road and he was funny, aloof and fit.

Anze didn't have that hold over me anymore, he wasn't as beautiful or charming these days. And either he'd got shorter or I'd got taller. Maybe that's what happens when someone loses their power over you: they look shorter.

Maybe recent years had been tough on him. I said to him, 'You look shorter' and he said to me, 'Well, you've put on weight.' I had!

We were flirting!

I asked him who his friend at uni was again, I couldn't remember his name. He was a friendly guy, an Asian fella on his course. It was doing my brain in that I couldn't remember his name. Anze said, 'I'm not telling you cos it's winding you up'... Again, more DELICIOUS flirting!

At the end of the night Anze was going to drive us back to his house, he'd moved from north to west London. On the way home, the police pulled him over. I was so drunk it hadn't occurred to me that he was drink-driving. They pulled him over and they said what's your name? And he said Frank. And I thought, OK, I didn't know Anze was short for Frank!

Luckily for him they said they couldn't be bothered with the paperwork of arresting him and he admitted when they went he would have been over the limit. Mad really. But we were nearly home, so on we ploughed, Anze and I.

When we got back to his house, I thought, Oh, they've downsized. But don't worry because he still lived with his mum. Anze had forgotten his keys so he woke his poor mum up at 3 a.m.

Now when I was going out with Anze, his mum was white. This guy's mum was black. So his mum was a whole different race and I still didn't twig.

I must have known somewhere within my body that this was not Anze because I did not want to sleep with him – at all. I ate all of his Jelly Tots and went straight to sleep. Thank God. I don't wanna sleep with no impressionist.

I made him drive me home the next day and explained to him that what he did was not cool at all.

He phoned me later that day to say we should go on a date and my friend Nicky was shouting in the background, saying, 'No, because you are a liar, a big fat liar,' and we put the phone down, laughing.

OK, he's leaving me for a wooden post, I guess. Well, she is thin and tan!

Yeah, I Guess I Am a Life-saver

And then there was Adam. Adam was lucky enough to be my boyfriend for a month or two in the noughties when I was about twenty-five (we think – why are you guys obsessed with age?). He was good-looking, a bit of a nutter and loved to get naked regardless of location or company. He came as a package, he had a best friend who was clearly in love with him and she hung around us constantly. I didn't trust him completely, and I didn't trust her at all, but they were always fun.

One night he had a party on the little houseboat he lived on. People were drinking, he'd done some pills and we were chatting on the outside deck – well, I was chatting and he was gurning – and then he just jumped overboard. My chat is that bad, he plopped over the side.

Thank God the tide was in otherwise he would have jumped on to rocks and really injured himself. Instead of death by rocks, he went for the option of drowning! Captain's Choice!

All the party-goers looked down with bemusement, classic Adam. There was a bit of laughter and speculation about how he would get back on to the boat. This excitement slowly turned to panic as we watched him splutter away, head bobbing under this sludgy Thames water.

I started shouting at him, but he wasn't listening, he was less and less able to function.

No one was making a move to go in and get him, and instinct and urgency took over. I emptied my pockets and jumped overboard.

I swam up to him and tried to prise his hands off the wooden post he had attached himself to. I put his arm around my neck and tried to reason with him. I wanted him to loosen his grip on the post and let me get him to safety. It was cold and dark and the water was swishing around with the current of the other boats. He told me to go away and that he was fine in the water. Quite often, especially in my twenties, I would take what people said at face value, thinking that I must have got it wrong and they must be right. So, for a second I thought maybe he's fine and I'm over-reacting and then I remembered he was a danger to himself *sober* let alone completely off his bonce. And he *was* absolutely out of his mind.

I wasn't expecting gratitude but I wasn't expecting aggression and hostility – on pills of all things? Practically impossible I thought, but maybe they'd worn off some time ago and he'd moved on to coke.

I tried to move his grip so I could help him. He barked, 'Leave me alone, I'm staying here.' I thought, OK, he's leaving me for a wooden post, I guess. Well, she is thin and tan!

It was quite dramatic: I tell him that this is serious and I need to get him to safety and I start to be more authoritative for once. I yank his hands away from his new friend and force them around my neck, sort of holding him and doggy paddling to the edge. The worst thing about it is the brown water, some of which you can't help but swallow in the chaos. What the eff is in this water? Bodies definitely and not the good ones (alive ones).

I get him to the boat and someone calls for an ambulance. Adam was fine and we both showered, trying to get the yuck out of our systems, trying to reset. The ambulance came and the people were very nice considering we were massively wasting NHS resources. Mind you, he got a tetanus jab because the water is so scummy and I didn't – even though we were both in it.

I should have asked for one but didn't want to bother them, and ultimately I was fine. He was bemused the next day and didn't remember most of it and we had a good old chuckle about the drama.

We only lasted about a month after that. We might have lasted longer but it coincided with a time when I was trying to clean up my act a bit and I had deduced that he wasn't exactly a tower of stability.

Pop a picture of a wolf on your pants, it works a charm.

I've Been Thinking...
About Your Personality

At this point, in my early twenties, I lived in a housing association house in Islington. **My friend Jules was in the mix of people living there – we were reunited again after university.** We found it easier to click back into our friendship because she had moved to London and I was drinking less and trying to get my life in order.

My friend Nicky also lived there. Nicky is exceptionally easy company; the most laid-back, porcelain-faced girl you've ever seen. She eats very slowly and knows every indie band from the twenty-first century.

I wasn't a daily drinker at this point. I was always trying different combinations to limit my drinking: sometimes I would drink every night but with no dramas and sometimes I would just drink three times a week, or I would go teetotal, but I was always *thinking* of booze and it wouldn't be long before I erupted in a massive bender and totally disgraced myself.

I've noticed other alcoholics doing that, too; they'll give up drinking and after a year, go back to it, thinking that this time it's different. But they don't go straight back out on a big bender – TOO OBVIOUS! No, they'll start off with shandies, or they'll leave some wine in the bottle… CASUAL! They might do this for a month and everyone whispers that maybe they are now OK. However, it's all so they can eke out the game for longer, they're just delaying the inevitable.

We lived in a four-storey housing association house that was crumbling down. My old school friends all went on the waiting list at the same time and, bit by bit, we managed to all live together in central London, at Leeds outskirts prices. It was such a bargain that I was able to save a bit for the first time ever. Sure, my bedroom ceiling caved in and nearly fell on my head, but that's actually very humbling!

A housing association is a scheme to give people cheap rent in areas which would usually price them out of the market. It's an excellent resource and should be bigger, although naturally some people abuse it. I was in one housing association house before the one with my friends, and the woman there had bought her own flat which she rented out and then she lived in the housing association house. WHICH IS ACTUALLY AGAINST THE RULES, MANDY, I did not say.

You sometimes get some unusual characters too. The other person I lived with in my first housing association house was a small forty-year-old man who was extremely paranoid. He smoked a lot of weed, worked night shifts and had a big picture of a wolf on his bedroom door to keep people out. I had never once set foot in his room, I did not dare, but, like I say, he was paranoid. Turns out he was onto something: pop a picture of a wolf on your pants, it works a charm – everyone has kept out of mine for ages.

In this new house with all my friends, initially there was an older alcoholic guy in there who was a big fan of absinthe. He was nice but once or twice he shat himself and another time, he fell through the trap door.[12] On the upside, he really highlighted to Jules that I was actually doing quite well, comparatively.

When he moved out, it was just me and my Broadstairs mates living there and it was really nice, there was a real sense of community. We went out to comedy and music gigs a lot, Nicky got all the latest CDs and brought them home, even though CDs were largely becoming defunct, we gorged on local Sunday dinners and watched the

---

12   Yes, we had a trapdoor.

house of impossibly fit guys across the road. Something for everyone (unless you were one of the lads being perved on). The summers were full of fun and laughter.

But every summer turns to winter[13] and in the winter the house was freezing and it never felt like you could scrub it clean because everything was so old. And then the mice moved in. One day Nicky found a mouse squished in her bed. Flattened dead. Too late for both of them. By the second winter I was quite miserable. I had let life grind me down. I used to be such a positive, happy kid, but slowly through the years, my inner compass had shifted to negative.

I was working for the corporate TV company in Chiswick, with the boss who owed people money. It was so far removed from what I wanted to do. I had to wear formal wear for shoots and watch some blustering CEO do seventy takes, talking about why health and safety was key to the company or some other total doody. There was more soul in a wet biscuit.

I was sending TV ideas off to production companies to see if they wanted to develop them – or develop me (and give me a job), but I wasn't getting anywhere.

One day I was moaning to Jules and she just lost it with me and said, 'I can't hang around with you, you're just so negative it does my head in.' I had already been told I

---

13   Not immediately, of course. I've seen a few springs and autumns in my time, don't worry about that!

was negative by other people, so the outburst really hit me hard, because I knew it was true. Your truest friends will be straight with you and that single statement put me on a path that I fully believe changed my life.

Jules and I had grown up together and we both knew the power of positivity and we knew about energy suckers and somewhere along the line, I had become one. That moment was a lightning bolt. And as annoying as it was, I needed to hear it.

In my mind, I had reasons to be negative: I hated my job, I didn't like myself and I was chubby and lost. But that's perspective. I could have flipped my perspective and thought, I'm young and healthy and I have friends and live centrally and the world is my oyster. But I didn't, until Jules broke the spell I was under.

Now, I didn't change my thinking overnight because that's quite hard to do, but I did set upon a ten-year exploration of trying to temper the mind. Actually, to be fair, I am still on it, as it's a lifetime's work. But I do feel like a completely different person.

I read books on positivity, I read more books, and then I got audiobooks, so that I could listen as I walked to the station. I went fully in. I tried to hypnotise my brain as I slept, just in case it worked (I mean that one was zero effort, so I thought I might as well – no idea if it did anything of course but worth a go). I did NLP, tapping and I got six weeks of free counselling. I monitored my thoughts more, and I made an effort to be more fun.

I tried so hard to re-educate my brain and look at things positively. I knew that it would change my life if I could do it. Heaven knows I'd read Richard Wiseman's *The Luck Factor*.

It's hard because you are trying to alter the neuro pathways that have cemented over years and years. But I knew if I wanted to have success and happiness and peace and joy, there was no other choice. Everything started with my thinking.

A lot of gaining confidence is of course just doing it and not being a little bitch!

How I Got into Comedy

Without this shift in thinking, there's no way that I would have thought of comedy as a career option. I didn't know anyone from my town or school or life who had gone into acting or comedy or anything like that, so it didn't occur to me that this could be a path for me. There were no comedy nights in Thanet growing up. It wouldn't have entered my brain. Except for a series of events, which did not seem like anything at the time, but you look back and connect the dots…

Nicky, Jules and I kept going to watch comedy at Up the Creek on a Sunday. Up the Creek is a fantastic club in Greenwich and we knew the promotor, Will, a tiny bit. My friend had a crush on him so we loved going down there.[14] I was buzzing afterwards from watching a show and being a part of the audience; all these people in one room laughing. It made me giddy with happiness. I saw Mark Watson MCing and couldn't believe how funny he was, how in the room he was. It was magic (but without all the dead white doves).

I was so clueless as to what live comedy was. After a few trips to Up the Creek, I saw an MC doing the same bit two weeks in a row. I felt duped. What? He's not making it up right now or writing a brand new twenty every week? I can't have really imagined that's what people did, could I? I've no idea. I just know that when I found out they didn't, I felt like I'd found them out. It must have set me thinking that if it's largely scripted, how hard could it be? Well, it turns out the 'scripting' is the hardest bit.

For my twenty-fifth birthday, I went to a comedy club in Islington with some friends. Matthew Crosby was MCing and he was funny. I was drunk and a bit extra, they made the mistake of talking to me and I really joined in. I was every comedian's nightmare – a gobby girl thinking she's adding to the night. I thought I was as funny as the comedians. Reader, I wasn't! Looking back, it was cringey behaviour, but it hopefully

~~~~~~~~~~

14 Will is now a friend and books me for some of the best gigs around.

makes me more empathetic now when someone does it to me.[15]

And the third thing that happened to set this fantasy in motion occurred at a music festival. Sally and I had made friends with these northern lads who were really fun and who worked in music, so they used to get us festival tickets for a summer or two. At one festival we didn't get the VIP wristbands and all our friends were getting free drinks in the special section with the nice toilets and the random celebs. So we decided to break in. We worked out a system: we just had to heave ourselves over a massive wall, scramble over the top, and then under another fence, which brought us out right by the ladies toilets, where we came face to face with the VIP girlies. They would be touching up their make-up and up popped a couple of moles 'HIIIIYA'. Once we were in there we would sometimes do a quick outfit swap, from mole to mademoiselle.

It was a pretty fun system, more fun than being given a wristband really. That was until one day Sally got stuck on the massive wall and was going to jump down but a security guard came towards her with about six guard dogs. Everyone was looking at her. I will never forget her face; she'd been caught, there was no styling it out, she was on top of a wall with no wristband and

---

15 Terms and conditions apply.

half a dozen dogs barking up at her. I was scared for her but also could not stop laughing. Luckily, because everyone was staring and she was obviously in an awkward situation, the man felt sorry for her and let her slip back down the other side, into obscurity.

Anyhow it was backstage at a music festival one year that people kept coming up to me to tell me how pretty Sally was. I couldn't figure out what they wanted me to do about it. Just tell her directly because when everyone was telling me, it made me feel like her security guard. Also, I was at that hellish age where everyone's looking for their identity. I didn't know who I was but I definitely wasn't the pretty one, that was Sally, and I wasn't the smart one, that was also Sally. So who was I?

Later that evening we got chatting to an older guy there who seemed to run the place. We didn't understand what he did but he seemed fun and he kept bringing us drinks so we were having a great time. We'd only been there an hour when naturally he chimes in with, 'Your friend is beautiful.' Well, yes obviously, I'd have to be blind and it turns out deaf to have missed that.

A bit later I was showing off, telling a story and he said, 'You're funny, you should do stand-up.' And there it was, a lightning bolt. Maybe *that* was my thing. It had never occurred to me to actually DO it myself until a man of all people suggested it. Maybe this made sense, comedy was the only thing I really, really loved. I later found out that guy went on to run Live Nation, who do a lot of big stand-up tours, and I've since worked for them.

It's worth noting that Sally is very funny too but she's had a stable enough childhood to not need to elicit laughter from strangers.

So the seed was sown.

By this time, I was starting to think more things were possible. I was working at Leopard TV in Islington, two minutes' walk from my house. They gave me a short contract which they kept renewing and I loved it there, it was by far my favourite TV job. And I had got it by sending off some ideas which they liked, so maybe I wasn't such a doofas after all. I was in the development team. We had to churn out ideas and my main boss, Bernard, was kind enough to help me learn how to write treatments. The cherry on the cake was sitting next to a very funny, sarcastic producer called Sharon, who would become a good friend. Maybe the positive thinking was working! And the mice were gone, too. I'm not saying I 'positively thought' the mice away, but maybe Rentokil did.

I had also more or less stopped yakking up after meals. I didn't want to ruin my teeth and so long as I could run a few addictions, I didn't need them all. I still had alcohol and now coming very soon... stand-up.

I plunged in and started a six-week stand-up course in Soho every Tuesday night. A lovely guy called Logan

Murray ran it. We learnt about our personas, and a bit about joke structure. We would read out our jokes to the class and get feedback. It was thrilling.

At the end of the six weeks, everyone had to do a five-minute set at a big showcase. I say a big showcase, it was made up of family and friends and was disarmingly supportive. I loved my first gig. I was so nervous, but I pulled it together and had a great time. So much so that I thought, This is going to be easy, and then died on my hole for about two years.

No, of course I had some good gigs, but I wasn't consistent. And it took me ages to find my voice, and then it turns out it's just the same one you use at home.

After doing comedy for a couple of years I managed to get on a sketch show for BBC Three and at the screening of that, I got my first agent! I remember my agent's assistant came to see me at a gig at the Albany in London. The feedback was that I needed to get more, OR ANY, style (I was wearing a black baggy polo neck and some bad jeans). And the other note was that I was very negative, on and off stage.

So I had come so far but I still had *a lot* of work to do!

The sketch show I had appeared on came and went without much attention and I was one of about twelve people in it so it didn't launch me anywhere. It would be another two years before I did anything on TV again and I just kept thinking I am not good enough and never will be. But I had no choice than to persevere – I really, really wanted to make it.

My agent couldn't get me any opportunities and I couldn't seem to get them for myself either. It was painful to want something so much and not feel like a natural – to see other people coming on to the scene confidently and getting opportunities immediately. I quit stand-up a few times but always went back to it because there was no better plan.

After some time I decided if I was really going to be all in, I needed to REALLY beat my number one enemy – ONCE AND FOR ALL – I had to beat my mind. This wasn't about thinking positively and smiling more; it was a bit deeper, fundamentally I had zero belief in myself. And that was the next big hurdle.

People say, 'You have to believe in yourself' or that you have to get rid of 'self-sabotage' but they never say HOW. In the end I decided to go for hypnotherapy and I had several sessions to make me more confident. I was lucky to get a good therapist who I clicked with. It wasn't a magic bullet but it certainly helped.

A lot of gaining confidence is of course just doing it and not being a little bitch! I worked hard on the stand-up, I said yes to every gig and I hustled for more. I would do a gig in Wales, get back at 3 a.m. and then get into work for 9 a.m. People always ask how to make it in stand-up and it really is just a case of writing lots and gigging lots, and dying on your ass lots. There is no shortcut, you learn through doing it. We are all full of excuses – 'there's no club in my home town' – set one up! 'People don't like weird stuff' – well then, find your audience! 'I'm too right wing' – well then, change your politics, etc., etc.

It's boring to say but I got into meditation a bit and slowly became more confident. This coincided with people opening up a bit more about female acts, so although it was way slower progress than I would have liked, it was mainly moving in the right direction. I still resented posh people who had confidence, I still resented the male-dominated industry, I still resented all the men who just hired men exactly like them, and I resented all the female producers who only got excited by the boys and kept the girls out, but as my confidence gradually built, my career very slowly started to ascend.

Guilt is such a waste of time. I was living in a body of guilt and he was living in a three-bedroom house he'd just bought with his new fiancée.

Am I Dying Through My Vagina?

The other thing that happened around this time was I met a guy who would go on to have a huge impact on me. He remains my longest relationship to date and we went through a lot together; we were instrumental in changing each other, I think for the better.

Nick (that was his name) told my friend recently that he picked me up in the morning one time and I had a load of beers and ciders and he thought, Oh dear, I've got a live one here. But I seem to remember he was quite hedonistic, too. He was coming towards the end of his flat tenancy and we smoked and drank in the flat and lived like kings (kings on a very low income).

I asked him if it was OK to smoke inside, he said you

can do what you like here, it's Nicky's place! When we would get cider and takeaways in and roll up snouts we would sing: 'Come on over to Nicky's place. Do what you want, it's that kinda space, yeah, come on over to Nicky's place.' Then he would roll another joint.

I went out with him for five and a half years and I was never fully sure we wanted the same thing but I knew he really loved me and I wanted to love him in the same way, but at the time I wasn't really capable of it.

He knew and could feel that my heart was closed. He said I would only let him in a bit. And one day he tried to talk to my heart to get it to open and he directly spoke to it; he told my heart that it was safe and it could open and trust him, and that he loved me. It sounds bonkers, but we both felt the energy of my heart physically opening. It was insane.

He texted me some time ago to say when he doubts the spiritual world, he reminds himself of that moment because it was palpable. He opened the fucker. Not fully but he left it ajar. Now I think my heart is open too much. It's just flapping in the wind. I think the best thing is to operate it like a cat flap with four different settings then you can shut it off when necessary.

I was single for over seven years after Nick. I've no idea why, maybe the guilt, maybe fear of getting in another relationship. Maybe – we're all thinking it – my personality?!

AM I DYING THROUGH MY VAGINA?

Lets just say that, honestly, I had to focus on my career. I split up with him because we were at a crossroads – marriage and babies or flourish in my career and I didn't think I could do both. The guilt of ripping someone's heart out is as bleak as it comes. I felt so bad even though he moved on and got engaged to someone else pretty bloody quickly. Guilt is such a waste of time. I was living in a body of guilt and he was living in a three-bedroom house he'd just bought with his new fiancée. Who, by the way, is a total babe. Good for you, I thought when I saw her.

About a year into my relationship with Nick I developed pain during and after sex. Once I even went to A&E because I thought I was dying from the vagina. They just laughed at me. I tried to explain that I have a high pain threshold and I wasn't trying to get attention (I do that by being vegan), but they were literally sniggering at me. Here is a timeline of my pain, and how long it took to work out what it was. 'Oh goody,' I hear you cry. No but this might be useful in case you have traditional lady's bits or sleep with someone with traditional lady's bits. I think it's interesting because no one talks about it, so I suffered for years, and now I'll slap it down here so hopefully you don't have to:

- I only started getting pain during sex about twelve months into a relationship with Nick. It wasn't every time, but enough to make me reticent about doing it. Sometimes after sex, I would be writhing around on the floor, sweating and yelping. And not in a sexy way, more in a bloated, wounded animal way.

- I went to a doctor to discuss it. He was an old-school guy, little rimmed glasses, his resting face was disapproval. His father was probably in the army. I told him it hurt a lot after sex and that I would like to get to the bottom of why. He said that a lot of women just don't enjoy sex and that maybe we are not built to enjoy it. So I said, 'My condolences to your wife, sir', flicked my hair, and spun on my heel. And by that I mean, I told him I didn't agree, said I would be off, and then accidentally walked into the door.

- I waited another year and approached another doctor. This time, I had private medical insurance through work (I was an executive PA. According to the contract). So luckily, or unluckily, I was packed off to see the 'best gynaecologist' in the country. He booked some tests and scans and eventually a laparoscopy, where they cut you open under a general anaesthetic and can have a look inside. Peekaboo!

- After all of these tests, months later, he said there was nothing biologically wrong with me and that it must be trauma-based. So the pain and stress around it continued for twelve years. I tried all sorts of healing therapy to get over anything in the past which may have been triggering it. I spent thousands of pounds and years' worth of anguish and worry. I felt guilty with any new partner that I couldn't be wild and free with abandon every time.

- And then at a routine scan recently, a nurse said, 'By the way, you have a retroverted uterus.' I asked whether this might be what was causing me the pain and she looked sad and said this was highly likely and that she had one, too.

WHY THE HECK DON'T GYNAECOLOGISTS KNOW ABOUT THIS? A QUARTER OF WOMEN HAVE IT – A QUARTER. And I gotta write about it in my book to try and let other people know.

That gynaecologist could have saved me twelve years of me thinking it was my fault and that it was solely from emotional damage if he had just done a basic two-second pelvic exam. He could have saved me being cut into. Or, if he'd looked properly in the laparoscopy, HE WOULD HAVE FUCKING FOUND THE RETROVERTED UTERUS and could have flipped it the other way, a sort of 'while I'm down there' scenario. But no, that clown is on over £300k a year and does not even know the basics.

I guess one good thing about male doctors not giving a shit about women's pleasure organs is that in a bid to fix the pain-during-sex issue, I did get therapy for things that had happened in the past; ya gross misconducts, ya sexual regrets, ya being raped.

I had an excellent sexual health therapist who did the previously mentioned EMDR for sexual trauma and it was incredible and free on the NHS, so swings and roundabouts. No, I don't WANT to discuss my retroverted uterus either, but hopefully it helps other people having the same issues. 'We came for the happy-ending story but we left with the retroverted uterus stuff.'

Not naming something is very powerful because you cannot claim ownership of that which has no name. That's why I learn all my boyfriends' names. So I can OWN them.

A Rose By Any Other Name

Speaking of women and their kit, something that boggles my mind is there is no word for the whole caboodle of the female anatomy. Vagina is not it. There is no word for the whole thing! We forgot to name the thing we all came out of.[16] We entered the world through this majestic vessel and then thought, No need to give *that* a name, I doubt they're gunna feature much in life.

Not naming something is very powerful because you cannot claim ownership of that which has no name. That's why I learn all my boyfriends' names. So I can OWN them. My friend just said there is a name for it:

---

16 Unless you are a gross little caesarean baby jk jk jk.

pussy. Well, yes, but imagine going into the doctor's. 'Have a quick look at my pussy could you?'

So as we don't have an official name for the whole thing I am going to make one up because heaven knows I'm going to be talking about them for a bit more. So I propose we call them CAROLS. Carol is a no-nonsense name, it's not sexy, it's not infantilising. Carol gets the job done. And also it reminds you of Christmas, which is nice, because 'pussies' are so good, if you get to be near one... IT'S CHRISTMAS!

Often female genitalia is presented by a male curator; people enjoy women's bodies when they are draped tenuously over a car or a man, or another woman. When they are giving pleasure, or delicately presented as an offering.

If women talk about the mechanics, and the raw, unfiltered power of our Carols, in all their blood, guts and gory glory, people tell us to pipe down. It's not the 'vaginas' they know. Or want to know. They want the sanitised version for *them*. But they belong to us. We take ownership of them by naming them and discussing them in real terms.

People don't like women talking about their bits – it's fine for men but people think it's unladylike for women. OK, but I can't think of anything more ladylike than a vaggginne.

So on that note, I will proceed to talk about my labia

if you don't mind. It's a bit XL. More to love. I went to one of my best friend's weddings once – you remember Sally from before. And the wedding was at a house, so people kept asking Sally admin questions and she thought, Wait a second, I'm the bloody bride here, why am I running around looking for Colin's umbrella and looking up ingredients for Celia? So she went upstairs for a little moment to herself (cry) and I tagged along with a couple of other besties. To cheer her up I said, 'Does THIS help?' and lifted my skirt up to show my pants. Evidently the pants were a weird shape and some of the old girl was elegantly hanging out. Well, she was as disgusted as she was delighted and it shocked her out of her upset, she laughed for a good five minutes.

Any time anyone's upset, I will use the same technique, 'Oh sorry that your cat's been run over – would you care to get an eyeful of this?'

I talked about my big labia in a stand-up show once. I mean it's not *that* big, I've never got it trapped in a lift OK? When I talked about it, sometimes men would wince. They would actually wince. What? Because a body part is a slightly different shape to what you see in porn?! Grow up.

Also, the rate at which labiaplasties are being performed on TEENAGERS is increasing, faster than many other procedures. This is a cosmetic surgery where they make your labia smaller, and it comes with a lot of dangers and complications. It's a risky surgery and young women are getting them. I do blame porn, because in porn they largely have the tucked-up ones. But with the bigger ones, you are getting more bang for your buck – so shut up and enjoy it. You shouldn't be complaining anyhow, it's rude to talk with your mouth full.

I have had women and girls with tears in their eyes thanking me for talking about this in a positive way. So it's worth me upsetting some prudes in order to get some merch sold. Sorry, I mean in order to connect with these women, tell them it's normal, lovable even.

So that's that taken care of (dusts hands) and now, PLEASE can we just talk about penises for a minute?!

Penises: you may have seen one, touched one, heard one… or, you may be lucky enough to have your own! Well, I think penis owners have just as much shame, but in a totally different way. And sometimes it's worse for men because they don't talk about things as much. And shame, like my ex, thrives in silence.

I think it's cheap, rude and nasty when people are mean about dick size. It's not like the owner can do anything about it, so it's just spiteful to torment them, and ironically, it just makes you look small OK????

All penises are beautiful. If you have a mini-p, just be honest, have the discussion. I've had some of the best sex of my life (thanks for asking) with a man with a medically small penis. And it was so good because he had a can-do attitude. He had read a book called *She Comes First* and he was mind-blowing at the hand and mouth stuff, so he could have put an earbud in there and I would've been ready. A lot of sex takes place in the mind, don't you know. Mind and clit, I guess, sometimes the kitchen, potentially in the Honda Jazz. But mostly the mind.

We put so much pressure on men's ding-dongs and then tell them not to live in male toxicity – OUTRAGEOUS. So, let's be nice to guys, whatever the size. Cue jingle!

A high proportion of the older crew think that working on yourself is self-indulgent, I think it's more self-indulgent to let all your pain spread out like a wildfire, burning everybody else in its wake.

What is Wrong With Your Face?

My parents' generation seem to feel silly spending too much time or money on the pursuit of happiness. I wish they knew that they were allowed to indulge themselves – it would have been better for them and their offspring.

Generalisation alert: I've found a high proportion of the older crew think that working on yourself is self-indulgent, I think it's more self-indulgent to let all your pain spread out like a wildfire, burning everybody else in its wake. They think they've saved money but we've just had to spend it on therapy instead.

When I was with Nick and doing a lot of work to try and make it in comedy, my life was beginning to feel a little more under control: sure, I was not *not* drinking, but I had largely stopped waking up in my own urine AND other people's! Plus, I wasn't drinking daily, it was more of a 'save it for best' scenario. I might only drink three or four times a week, but I would really try and make it count! Get a lot down my gullet and then try not to drink the next day.

I had booked my first proper stand-up TV appearance. If you don't include the stand-up I did on Nuts TV, which I don't because it was five minutes on a channel no one knew existed.

This was proper TV, it was *Russell Howard's Good News* and a lot of people watched it and I was nervous as heck. I did so many gigs to drill the set, but I was also still worried about my mum at the time.

Throughout my life my mum was a light sleeper and had a lot of allergies and was always coughing with asthma at night. So I learnt to be very quiet as a child, I can close a door like a ninja. If ninjas even close doors. I would look up supplements and remedies to help with her hair or confidence, or practical things to aid her asthma and allergies. The latter two sometimes being very debilitating. When I would stay over I would hear her coughing through the night and it would break my heart to see a bin of tissues by the bed each morning. Her asthma definitely got worse when she was upset or stressed. Sometimes, she seemed allergic to life itself. But when her sister died she could barely walk and her breathing was so shallow; if 'breath is life', she was more on the death side of things.

I took her to Egypt for a week so that she could have some heat in her lungs (the recommended treatment in 1840), and it seemed to do her the world of good, and it's a week I will always treasure. We only fought once – she told me to move my plate closer, and I said, 'Stop trying to control everything!' She burst into tears and said she didn't know she was so awful. Fighting once in a week for a mother and daughter on holiday alone is bloody good work, I think. It was a lovely holiday and when she got some sun on her bones, she was able to up the speed a bit. She was always better company when there wasn't a man complicating things. So often the way... Nah, I'm only kidding, I love guys, in fact I've got a couple of dicks in the old gob as I type!

She was very supportive about my upcoming gig on Russell Howard too and she wanted me to do well, encouraging me to go and run the set and enunciate. I've been lucky that bar a few exceptions she has been very supportive about my career, even though I have disgraced her in front of the gardening club and some family friends.

I was always in search of something to help alleviate Mum's asthma and the emotional issues behind it. And to be fair to the old bird, she would usually try them once or twice, often with incredible results, but then she wouldn't go back because 'the effects wore off'. Of course the effects wear off, you have to maintain it, you don't go to the gym once and then you're buff forever.

The things I would book for her were usually under the big, old, mistrusted umbrella labelled 'alternative health'. There's so much amazing work being done in this field. People get so suspicious and annoyed about alternative health and 'charlatans' but some medicine is the biggest ruse out there. People are making billions, while some medications are unnecessary or have side effects, or need to be counteracted with yet more drugs, and sometimes by treating the symptom people never get to the cause, and the health issues just manifest somewhere else.

Now, I am not denying that medicine can be terrific and lifesaving and actually I am a big fan. I use it, baby! But there shouldn't be such a divide, an either/or. I mean it's called 'complementary' medicine for a reason. Complementary or alternative health is not without its issues, and of course there are some quacks out there, but it's great when it treats the root cause and when it gives autonomy back to the individual.

I mean we know that people get headaches from stress, we know that periods often stop after a trauma, and we even know that there are cases of people dying from heartache[17] shortly after a loved one passes away, so

---

17   OK, you might call it a heart attack, sure.

to think that the body, mind and spirit aren't inextricably linked sounds, to me at least, madder than cheese.

Of course it's not that simple and babies are born with leukaemia, and young kids get sick and there's nothing anyone can do about it, and that's the most horrific thing in the world. And of course I'm not saying if I had cancer I would cure it with a flower remedy! I just think for stress-induced diseases where the medical world does not have the answers, some incredible work is being done with measurable results in complementary medicine.

I once had insane eczema all over my hands and couldn't bend my fingers. Then I got it over just ONE side of my face – exactly straight down the middle.

I was working at a private healthcare company at the time and a new CEO had just taken over and was making lots of redundancies. I was super-stressed because I had to schedule in these meetings and then watch people get their P45s.

I looked up what skin conditions on the hands and face meant in my medical journal, and by that I mean my spiritual book, and it said:

- Eczema on the face: 'the inability to face life'
- Eczema on the hands: 'the inability to handle life'

As soon as the meetings stopped, the eczema vanished. I realise these things can be a symptom of diet too, and allergies of course, and everyone's different – but all I'm saying is, emotional toxins have an insane effect on the body.

I think many of us realise now that as fantastic as medicine is, it is still limited, and even doctors are attributing diseases to loneliness, stress or unresolved trauma. One doctor I read about suspected that a lot of her patients' health issues were down to loneliness, so she used her bookings system to set people up secretly in the waiting room. She scheduled the appointments of the people she wanted to set up back to back so they would meet in the waiting room. She was doing it for ten years and had THREE MARRIAGES. I mean, sure, my source here is Twitter's Fesshole, but I like to think it's true.

Justine thinks if you believe enough you can do anything. But if I believed I could be a gymnast or an astronaut, at this stage, it would still be very slim odds.

Geoff Leopard

Don't worry, although I was getting into a lot of spiritual stuff, I was still a massive chump. As demonstrated by the fact I was in Geoff Leopard, 'the worst band in the world', a lovely quote from our friend's dad.

Maybe you've heard of us? We were pretty big (dress sizes). I'll tell you a few stories from the band days, but first, I need you to picture the band, so let me outline the members:

Justine was on keys – she effed her very young keyboard teacher and so stopped her lessons quite early, and she duly remained terrible. She wore tiny gold lamé shorts that hugged everything. You could see the outline (and the inline) of her Carol™ but she didn't care. Justine is a one-woman institution. She has the confidence of an army and is fizzing with energy. She once performed the whole of the rap from KLF''s 'Justified and Ancient' to Rio Ferdinand at a work event. Everyone looked at the floor and asked her not to do it again. I've not met anyone who gives less of shit. She's a force to be reckoned with, but often she will be marching uphill in totally the wrong direction. Justine also often misses the joke and takes everything sincerely at face value. She's barking mad and beautifully sincere. For the first year she didn't get that we were a joke band, and that we HAD to be a joke band because we were just so bad. Justine thinks if you believe enough you can do anything. But if I believed I could be a gymnast or an astronaut, at this stage, it would still be very slim odds.

Sally's (the same one from before, don't you know) nickname was Bang Bang – on account of her drum playing – she was a more choosy lover than the name would suggest. She picked up the drums quite easily, she picks up anything she's interested in, and she's got the kind of face you can trust. Or as one shopkeeper said to her once, 'You have a very nice open face.' She thanked him, and then he said, 'I would quite like to cum across it.' Anyhow, I digress... Sally is very good value, the anchor of the group in a lot of ways, extremely funny and always has some big ideas. She tried to persuade us to come into a festival gig in someone's garden in a helicopter, but we were quite skint at the time so couldn't cough up all that money for one joke. Sort of wish we had now.

But we downscaled to an ice-cream van which we all burst out of.

We were eating so many mini flakes from nerves (like Beyonce I imagine) before we went on, the ice-cream vendor billed us £50 for 'sundries'. It's not £50, Neil. He was also selling ice creams while we were on, which was against the festival rules as it was outside food, so we ended up shouting at him from the stage, saying, 'It's for charity, Neil, you cunt. Stop selling ninety-nines.' Which come to think of it might explain the sundries bill.

Ruth was on lead vocals and guitar. Now Ruth is a blonde-haired, big-tittied rock chick – she looks amazing and is great company, but she would never know it because she tends to go out with guys who ebb away at her confidence. She could actually play the guitar and sing like an angel. She is an angel. If she'd been single from birth she'd know this.

Magdalin was on bass, and quite often she would purposely forget her bass. I think that tells you what you need to know about Magdalin. She was a brilliant realist. Magdalin is deadpan and excellent. But we dragged her there.

Me: Loulie. Everyone could sing fifty times better than me but I was the lead singer because I would swing from things and roll around the floor. I put on a show, but I had to get so drunk to overcome my shyness (and the fact that I couldn't sing for shit).

Weirdly, we played Surfstock festival twice. My favourite time was when we rode down in a minibus with an Australian band who were so much fun; we met them all through a mate and they really matched our energy. They were loud, funny and keen to throw themselves into trouble.

I found and hired the minibus and Sally and I drove to Cornwall and back. No great calamities, aside from pranging the van a bit. Oh, and Magic (one of the best-looking Australian guys) suddenly went missing after a petrol-station stop. We drove about ten miles before we noticed he wasn't in the van and turned back around, only to find him spread out sparko on the floor by the newspaper stand. He'd passed out drunk and rolled out the back of the van. Whoopsie.

When we got to the festival, we got straight amongst it, rampaging backstage to see who we could find. It was a very small festival but they had managed to snag The Gossip, so we were really excited about Beth Ditto being there. Justine immediately made friends with her and we set about getting as hammered as possible.

The security guards didn't love our vibe and tried to turf us out of the backstage area. There was a bit of a power battle between them and us and they were being quite hostile. Now, I get that as, to be fair to them, we must have been unbearable. I don't think they were spectacular to be fair, but we come out way worse in this story. I had forgotten a lot of the details of this, but the girlies filled me in. This, as silly as it sounds, is exactly what happened (backed up by four Geoffs and an event organiser):

I had forgotten my towel, so I said to Sally, 'If I tackle that security guard, can I have your towel?' Sensing some fun to be had, she immediately said yes.

Never one to shirk on a dare when I was drinking, I ran like a rhino at this guy's legs, there was a scramble between him, me and another security guard, and in the kerfuffle, we stole his walkie-talkie. We ran back to our tents, laughing hysterically. We knew one of the guys was called Steve, so we kept using the walkie-talkie to radio in things like 'Erm, Steve has anyone seen my protein shake?' 'Steve, I want to open up about my emotions.' 'Steve! I think I've killed one on the path outside, what shall I do?'

After a bit of high jinx from us we were met with: 'Geoff Leopard, we have GPS trackers on that radio and are coming for you!' They didn't of course, these were your rudimentary old-fashioned walkie-talkies.

One of my best friends from Broadstairs, Georgie, was working on another of our other friend's food stall. She was putting another toastie together, and was chuckling away at messages coming through the coms from the security guards: 'We need to find Geoff Leopard and get them out now. Now. And they are not performing!'

WHAT'S THAT LADY DOING?

By this point we were by our tents and had met a guitarist from another (proper) band. We told him what we were doing and he loved the chaos of it and joined in. We were having a grand old time with the walkie-talkie and our new best friend.

His band were due on stage in the following hour, and he suggested Geoff come on too and dance around for the opening song. We did not need to be asked twice.

Unfortunately when he told his bandmate, his band-mate said, 'Absolutely no way are Geoff Leopard coming anywhere near this stage and how the fuck are they still going?' Or words to that effect.

Now this was because about a year before, our band had organised a private party in a recording studio and invited all of our friends. The catch? They would have to listen to some of our songs. However, the editor at *NME* had listed the gig in *NME* for a joke.

We knew the editor and all thought it was kind of funny to put the shitest band in *NME* as an in-joke for a handful of people. We loved it. Until the owner of the recording studio saw it and told us we had to now move the party, because it had been listed as a public gig and he didn't have that sort of licence.

He kindly helped move us to a pub around the corner called The Macbeth.

This was where good bands on the way up played.

We turned up in ripped wedding dresses and big make-up. We couldn't play our instruments or sing and we played songs like 'Gas, Gas It's my Fuel – Fill Me Up, Baby I'm A Coming for You' and 'Rock is a Four Letter Word'. The sound guy was livid; he couldn't understand how we were so bad and why the crowd was lapping it up. He didn't realise we knew 80 per cent of them.

He pulled the plug on us early and the crowd started booing him. He must have been so confused as to how his reality could distort so wildly.

At some point we went downstairs to the basement and accidentally walked into the wrong room and saw him getting sucked off by the burlesque dancer, who was dressed as an astronaut. Maybe it's *not* so hard to be an astronaut?

Anyway, it was the same guy who was now in a band playing Surfstock and telling his bandmate that Geoff were not welcome. What are the chances?! Well we didn't need to dance for the boys, we had our own much smaller gig thank you!

Although I still wanted to do it. In fact, Sally and Magdalin were knocking back so much booze because I was trying to get everyone to rush the stage when these lads were on, and understandably they didn't want us to. Ruth and Justine were totally game. Luckily the security guards caught us first. They stole my Tesco bag with my show outfit in (every little helps), ripped off our wristbands and marched us unceremoniously to our stage to perform.

They glared at us throughout the set. If I was them I would have been cross too, but I probably would have cracked a bit of a smile. I mean, the state of us:

Sally had a doll strapped to her and they were wearing the same outfit. Magdalin was dressed as a strongman, but the only chest plate we could get was a Caucasian one and she is black, so she wore it and whited up her face. Pretty funny. A hilarious take on things, especially as at this festival we had seen two white people blacking up – WHAT THE EFF. This was circa 2007 and it was not OK. Their argument was that they were dressed as the guys from the film *Cool Runnings*. Yeah, but no boys. NOT *Cool Runnings*.

Ruth went as a leopard, and Justine went as 'the girl who rides the horse'. I was supposed to be the ring-master but the carrier bag the security guard stole had my top hat and jacket in. I never got it back actually and I think that was fully deserved, all things told.

The drama with the security guards had meant we were late for the gig and we ended up headlining, so there were quite a few people there. I can't help thinking they must have been disappointed, but the Australians helped the atmos by jumping around and throwing the flowers on stage, which Princess[18] had generously bought from the service station on the way down.

Sally was so drunk she passed out on the drums mid-set. She was literally out cold in the middle of the gig.

At one point, I was swinging from the lighting rig, and that's when the sound guy cut us off. However, the man who was running this tent made them put us back on. He was dressed as the rabbit from *Alice in Wonderland*, and we are pretty sure he was on crack.

It wasn't exactly Live Aid but it passed the time.

I wouldn't act like that now but those days were fun. It was really nice to be a part of something, to be in something together. A lot of my life I've craved a sense of belonging. I found it hard to trust people, and I hold friends to high standards so if any of them let me down, I just want to run away. I have sometimes found that, friendships can be transient, or scary, or take too much work, but in the band there was an ease. I trusted them *and* they were fun, and we were all working towards the same goal... making God-awful music.

---

18 A nickname of one of the gorgeous spirited Aussie lads.

Jazz in your pants once in the osteo office, shame on them, jazz in your pants twice in the osteo office, then it's shame on me.

Where Did You Learn to Jazz?

Most of my 'shames' from the past are simply anecdotes now and they don't hold the same resonance. Because I've changed the way I act, I feel like a different person, so the shame eventually dissipates. I mean I hate to gloat, but it's been years since I've tried to cop off with a married boss thirty years older than me, and an age since I've given myself a black eye from headbutting a plant pot. Girl Boss much?!

Now, most of my past shameful moments are quite funny to me, like getting barred from my cranial osteopath's practice because when he touched my head, I jazzed in my pants. Twice. Jazz in your pants once in the osteo office, shame on them, jazz in your pants twice in the osteo office, then it's shame on me.

I didn't tell him obviously, but he knew. Maybe because I walked out of the place like a duck. Actually, I think he knew because he was magic. Case in point, he made my box erupt by touching my foot. And they say magicians aren't sexy!

In fairness it wasn't his fault, he wasn't trying to test my Carol™. But equally, it wasn't my fault either, sometimes chi / energy / Carols™ have their own life force. Although that is not an adequate excuse for an affair, sorry.

I did then ask him if he wanted to go for a drink and that's when he barred me. But I swear he was the one telling me about his divorce and being weird with me. Barred me cos you were obsessed with me, did ya, babe? A story as old as time. Yep, every time anything bad happened to me, I was like, oh, they wanted it. Got locked out of my bank account – they wanted it. Nearly got run over – they wanted it. Got mugged – you guessed it – they wanted it!

Yes, happily, I tend not to get myself into compromising situations these days. I've given up getting the afore-mentioned happy endings in massages, bad-choice one-night stands, AND chucking myself at indifferent men (and there's so many of them, so well done me)! The good news is it only took about thirty-five years to get here. So keep dreaming, sisters!

Obviously I still have the same baseline personality, so life is not without scrapes. And no regrets about most of the past, you learn not to touch the hot plate by touching the hot plate.

Shame is ancestral and communal, it starts early and runs deep. I know, I know, she keeps banging on about shame, but it's actually really important guys! It drives people to kill their children to fit in (usually the girls, granted, so not *as* important), but still, we must dissolve shame at any cost because it's at the heart of addiction, depression and suicide. I try to absolve my shame by owning up to things and talking about them on stage, or here in this very book. So maybe you could do it at *your* work, whatever industry you are in – just go for it: start your presentation with a lighthearted anecdote: 'Hello, this is Angela and welcome to my talk on Network Rail. But first, a light anecdote about how I shat myself in Center Parcs.'

The media peddles a culture of shame, taking extracts of stories or sound bites without context, and blowing them up and targeting people for sometimes naff all. It's absolutely bonkers. Like a pack of wolves over someone's sound bite from *Loose Women*. I try not to buy into the muck, but of course sometimes I do.

◆ ◆ ◆

When I started comedy, my mum was of the opinion that 'nice girls' don't talk about certain things. I was on this TV show a while ago, and she said, 'Lemme tell your

Uncle Quentin.' And I said, 'Well maybe don't tell Uncle Quentin, because for a large portion of the show, I'm talking about my labia.' And she said, 'Lou, why have you got to do that?' And I said, 'I really just think it's a case of… supply and demand.'[19]

However, since then Mum and I have had some enlightening chats about women discussing their bodies, double standards and shame, and she's become quite progressive, which was always in her anyhow but it's lovely we are able to discuss it and listen to each other.

It's complicated because I think we should be able to talk about what we like, but then if we are always being rude with no depth there's not a lot to latch onto. If anyone is barking about their bits with no nuance, point, or fantastic joke, then yes, its low-hanging fruit of course – like my labia, etc., etc.

I'm trying to be less rude in stand-up, but now and again I think it's funny; as with anything in life, it comes down to context and nuance. My sweet spot is to do some gorgeous think pieces, natty observations, some astute commentary on life, and then throw in a little something-something about your father's perineum and ball sack. Something for everyone. And at the same time so much for no one.

---

19 They cut all the labia stuff anyhow, so that was a wasted conversation.
They always cut the labia stuff. Well guess what? This is my book so it's labia-heavy – just like me!

The thing I find interesting is that we often try to socially dictate who can talk about what, and often these things are loaded with social biases. Surely everyone should have the authority to talk about their own body in whichever way they choose.

I'd love the world to run free, shameless, blameless and painless. Obviously if you have done something irresponsible though, you do need to clear it up, apologise, learn from it, forgive yourself and then move on. But THEN do run naked 'n' free in the local cornfields. 'SORRY, FELICITY – MY BODY IS NOT BOUND BY SHAME!' 'Yes, I do understand but my family don't want to see your bits swinging around at this baby shower.'

Sometimes dreams do come true but sometimes, if you are a true visionary, you can turn that dream into a nightmare just like that!

Wine Head and a Slippery Slope

So I was doing all this work on myself, jazzing myself off in the cranial osteopaths and what not, but after nine years on the circuit while working other jobs at the same time, things were not moving as fast as I wanted.

I wanted success so much and I knew that having a reputation as a boozehound wasn't helping, but then I would look at someone like Johnny Vegas and think, Ah, maybe it's OK to do both. After a series of gaffes, there were two big events which hammered home that I could not, in fact, do both.

The first one was at Mach festival, a delightful comedy event in Wales run by the fantastic Henry Widdicombe. It's set in the sleepy, picturesque hills of Machynlleth –

the friendliest town around. People tend to go for the weekend and the place is so tiny that you bump into the same people in the street or at shows and bars.

I had come straight from LA to Wales, so I was worried about getting jet lag. I decided to outfox the jet lag by popping some diet pills I'd picked up in La La Land. A lovely little speed-based pick-me-up. Great – now I could drink more. I was in such good form, I even had some of my friend's zoot – I never usually smoked, but hey, I was in a great place with my self-prescribed mega mix-up.

I skipped off to do a mixed bill show with Arthur Smith, Rachel Parris and Ed Gamble. Weirdly, the cocktail of ingredients didn't really bring out my best side and I was an absolute psychopath. Arthur Smith, for anyone who doesn't know him, is about sixty-five years old, and a smashing guy. I pulled his trousers down (I know, I know, imagine a man doing that), I hurled factually incorrect abuse at Ed Gamble, who is actually a pretty perfect guy, and I threw an empty bottle of wine at the audience. I mean I could have seriously damaged someone. I think about that a lot and how differently it could have panned out. I feel so lucky I didn't hurt someone. What is the most expensive bottle of wine in the world? The one that takes someone's life away! (Puts hands on hips, pouts and raises an eyebrow while THAT sinks in.) I guess I just quiz-riddled you!

Some people left, some people complained and some people who had bought tickets to my show, which was on the next day, asked for refunds.

After the gig, the lush sketch group, The Birthday Girls, and the lush one-man band, Brett Goldstein, took me back to the house we had rented, which was about thirty minutes' taxi ride away. They all missed out on their big Saturday night because of me. I think they were scared to leave me because they seriously thought I had brain damage. I was speaking in tongues and trying to light the oven with the gas button only. There was no lighter and no food to put in it. I just kept clicking the button, shouting, 'Pizza, pizza, pizza… I'm going to cut you.'

Brett also had to accompany me to the toilet and wait for me while I made all sorts of noises and all sorts of fluid came out of me. What a friend he's been over the years.

The next day I was mortified and we lay in bed and read some abusive Tweets about me. I was crushed about drunk me, and Brett was very supportive but, as ever, he gently suggested I give up alcohol.

The next day, I did my show immensely hungover. I had to sit on a stool like an old alpha Canadian comic who wears checked shirts and always has one bottle of beer in his hand. I addressed the previous night's drama, although the crowd all knew anyway, because word had got around and also some of them were there.

I got through my show and felt well enough to go to the final night of dancing, which is always in a big circus tent, with various comics doing DJ sets for everyone to dance to. Lots of people were asking me about the night before. I tried to laugh it off as if I thought it was funny, but I could see people's faces and they didn't think it was funny. And nor did I.

I remember my friends Celeste and Matthew saying, 'You don't need to drink, you're really fun without it.' They both had a concerned look on their faces. And while I couldn't give it up for good, yet, it must have gone in the memory bank and helped for when I was strong enough.

◆ ◆ ◆

The second work trip of disasters was a snowboarding one. I asked the booker if I could do a ski festival. It was in Austria and you do gigs in the evening and board or ski in the day. Everything's paid for and you even come back with a few hundred squid. Lovely stuff. I was so happy to go – I love to board, I love to gig, I loved to drink. Sometimes dreams do come true and sometimes, if you are a true visionary, you can turn a dream into a nightmare very easily.

I was with a bunch of absolute smashers – they liked to drink more than me, so I thought I would be very safe, camouflaged even, to really indulge.

However, one fateful night, we were at high altitude, which increases the effects of alcohol, and I hadn't had dinner and I had drunk a lot of free wine. I did my set and that seemed to go well, but then it suddenly hit me: I was absolutely gone. A beast had been unleashed.

Why can some people be normal and chill and I go full honey monster? I heckled the other acts, started rowing with everyone and brought a mean guy back to my room. No one spoke to me the next day and I left the resort a day early. When I asked the booker where my fee was three months later he said, 'Are you out of your fucking mind?' and I said, 'Yep, fair enough, you keep that for damage limitation.' I knew I had to quit drinking. I thought, There's only one thing I like more than booze, and that is success. I knew I wouldn't have both afforded to me. Thank God.

I KNOW I SOUND LIKE YOUR ANNOYING RELIGIOUS EDUCATION SUPPLY TEACHER! But do know that I have fun socks on!

How I Stopped Drinking

Gigs were going quite well most of the time, so I couldn't understand why I wasn't a regular on TV and one day I asked my friend who was on TV a lot. She had complimented me after a gig and I'd said, 'If I'm funny, why can't I get on TV much?' And God bless her she was 100 per cent honest and just said, 'Producers don't trust you, you're too chaotic and you're a risk. They don't want that, they want a safe bet.' That really stuck with me and helped me, alongside the ski trip disaster, to quit alcohol forever.

I had to make money, I had to break through, I had no other back-up plan.

I knew people in my industry thought I was an alcoholic. I was tired of the pain and the shame. I was tired of not being in control. I had quit drinking before, but always gone back to it. This time felt different. This time I felt stronger in myself and it was non-negotiable, I had to do it.

I read a great book called *The Easy Way to Stop Drinking* by Allen Carr (not that one). It somehow made me realise that I wasn't missing out, in fact, I would only be missing out if I started drinking again. That was a game changer for me. It also detailed an experiment where some participants thought they were drinking alcohol when in fact they were given a placebo, but they started fucking and fighting anyway. This proved to me that while I wanted to use alcohol to help me let go, maybe I was chasing a release that didn't come directly from alcohol.

This sounds ridiculous, but I also got into exotic teas and really liked the rituals around making them. It gave me something to focus on. I bought into the idea they could change your state. I mean how much can a berry botanical really eff you up? But you go along with these things – mind over matter. And it does help. My friend knew a Chinese tea dealer so we went straight in with some high-end fare and I thought, Blimey, this is absolutely getting me off my tits – forgetting of course that we'd done some magic mushrooms before the tea ceremony. I also wrote an article in *The Guardian* to reclaim my drinking and to draw a line under it. That was cathartic, but it also felt like an announcement, so there was no going back. I guess you could do the same with your family newsletter or stick a blog up in your local coffee shop, it's all the same. Intention and declaration.

A month after I wrote the article, I was in Italy for a few days for a wedding (labia out of course). The day after the ceremony, I went to a seaside town alone, and I was watching people drinking as if it was the most normal thing in the world. I really wanted a drink – I mean no one would know, I was on my own – but I thought about the article and the people who had reached out to me saying how much it helped them get sober, and I had a mocktail instead.

Every time I wanted a drink I fast forwarded to what that would look like in the future, because it is never just one drink. I linked drinking with shame and I desperately wanted less shame not more. It got easier bit by bit. Someone once told me the more you do of something, the easier it gets and that's certainly true with sobriety. Plus, the longer I went not drinking, the more I could see improvements to my life.

I had been sober for about four months when a producer I knew a little bit said I should come to this fellowship meeting with her. She had read *The Guardian* article and this group had really helped her, so she wanted to bring me in. I said I didn't need it thankyouuuuuuu, I was a lone wolf.

Now, this group I'm referring to doesn't like publicity

(attraction not promotion, they say), so I won't say its name, but let's just say you might find it at the beginning of the phone book!

One reason they discourage people from celebrating them is because if someone then relapses it looks bad. People love to lament, 'I knew it – it doesn't work.' Maybe people are willing things to fail so they don't have to try them. As the old adage goes: 'Ask me to do anything but change.'

In my experience, the programme does work if *you* work it. It's like exercise: if you stick to it, it works. But you have to turn up.

Of course we are human beings, we're messy and self-destructive. There's no magic pill, nor should there be, the learning and the growth are the whole point. I KNOW I SOUND LIKE YOUR ANNOYING RELIGIOUS EDUCATION SUPPLY TEACHER! But do know that I have fun socks on!

I love the unnamable meeting because of its simplicity. You follow the steps, you get better. Plus, people who have no money can go. And no one's in charge, so it can't tip over into a cult (believe me I've tried)! It's egalitarian; they share out the roles and move them around. It's not status or money oriented, everyone's equal. I've seen people at meetings treat homeless people the exact same way as celebrities. I was livid: 'Hello, why are you talking to that bum? I've been on *QI*!'

HOW I STOPPED DRINKING

The first time I went into the rooms, years before the nice lady suggested it, I was not ready to give up. I went to one meeting, looked around and thought, I'm not like these losers. I'm too young and too cool to be an alcoholic! Ermmm, OK Timothée Chalamet. They say look for the similarities not the differences. The ego looks for separation to feel important and the soul looks for unity, and I'll give you a clue as to where I was... right up my ego's ass.

This time I knew it was important to go to the meetings because I was so bloody resistant. I knew I had to because of how much I didn't want to. The first meeting is so scary, and I do not know why. I think it's because you are declaring in front of others that you can never drink again and if you do drink again, you cannot lie to anyone about why you're drinking: you are drinking because you are an alcoholic.

Standing up in a room full of people and saying your name followed by the statement that you are an alcoholic is powerful. Words are powerful. Intentions are powerful. You declare it, and just like that you are in another dimension. It's like saying to a long-term partner, 'I want to break up.' You're changing paths with no map. You're flinging yourself out of a moving train. And yet it is the best thing I have ever done.

You see this as a loss, but that's because you don't have all the gains yet. If I could take people's hands and show them all the delicious treats and all the joy and peace that slowly unfolds if they get on to that path, they would leap on to it. But they have to take those first steps and they are quivering. And they don't quite believe you because they've never experienced it.

I cried for the first twelve meetings. And the rest! There's something so powerful about being in a room full of people all wanting to change. It's almost like something is in the room with you all, willing you on.

Rarely do you get to be with people all being fully present for an hour with the sole intention of getting better. It's sometimes so still in there. And the humanity. People, all humbled by life, all willing the best for each other and speaking from the heart with very little ego. That is so rare and so beautiful.

Once I went to a meeting in Oxford at Easter, and there was a fifty-year-old woman who shared with such warmth and gratitude. She said she came to the area twenty years ago, she had no family, she hadn't been on holiday for twenty years and everything she owned was in one carrier bag. Through doing the steps, her life was unrecognisable and she was truly grateful for everything she had.[20]

I thought stopping drinking was all I needed to do, but these meetings helped me with resentments and anger

20 Some of these details have been changed for confidentiality's sake, but you get the idea (it was actually a little monkey in Spain).

and getting mentally sober. Thinking about it, I should go back more.

I do think it's the best way to get sober but sometimes people aren't ready for it. My friend got sober initially by listening to a podcast about sobriety. And then went to a fellowship. Another friend had a wake-up call when someone died of liver disease, so he popped off to rehab. And someone else I know is still drinking even though her teeth have started falling out. So, yes, sometimes we hit snooze on the blaring alarm of life.

Being friends with sober people helps. Replacing the addiction with a better, healthier addiction is useful: climbing, skating, cold-water swimming – something that gives you a buzz.

I love not drinking now. I love the clarity and simplicity of it, but it's taken a long time to get here, via many, many mistakes. I used to think I was missing out, so inevitably I would always, slowly, creep back to the vodka. If I feel like drinking now, I just think about what that would look like a month on, and it would look like me losing everything I have fought so hard to get.

The word sober sounds so serious. I still love dancing till 1 a.m. and talking shit. I hang out with big drinkers and I still love all the enjoyable things I did drunk, but there's choice and power in my decisions now. And way, way less shame.

There's a freedom in ageing, like on the last night of a holiday in a far-flung destination, you know you're going home tomorrow, so go hell for leather, love. WILD ABANDON.

Death is a Strong Word, We Should Call it Recycling

Death is happening to us all, so I guess we have to get on board with it.

I did DMT once. DMT is the drug that's in every living thing and when you take it, it's supposed to replicate what happens when you die. And I took a shit tonne of it with a shaman in Archway. Archway is in north London and a shaman is someone who is like a spiritual teacher. Mind you, this one was also an actor in *Holby City* too, so you tell me.

After I came round from the DMT, he said, 'Never in my life have I seen someone dribble so much.'

And I looked down at my vest, which was absolutely sodden from my mouth fountain.

Anyway, this experience did actually make me a lot more comfortable with death. Not the dribbling. And the whole part where you see yourself dying isn't ideal – it's so real, you're panicking, you're thinking I'm dying, I'm really dying, Mum is going to be very upset indeed! It's very scary letting go of the ego… letting go of everything you think is in this material world. But then you are transported into another plane of existence (via some aliens obvs).

The aliens whizzed me around and I thought, Yeah, I've been here before of course I have, I know this, we're all from here. A bit like if you go and see your old childhood home, or a prominent ex in the same cologne, it all comes flooding back.

At one point I saw Indian dancers and there were symbols and hieroglyphics coming towards me. I didn't have a thinking analytical brain but it was as if my body was downloading these ancient characters and I understood them. My body knew what to do with them, in the way that a kitten just knows to chase a feather.

Then as the DMT was wearing off, I felt myself floating back down to earth but I didn't want to leave this heavenly world of pure love. I couldn't stop it though, the DMT was fading and the portal to this other dimension was closing. As I was dropping back down to the sofa in Archway, I heard a voice telling me that this human experience has to be about helping one another, that was the one big message. Jeez, I must set up that charity and adopt some children.

As I came back into my body, my ego was unfolding again. I started thinking, Where am I? Who am I? And why have I got a wet bib around me?

I don't think we should know when we die. No thanks, leave a bit of sweet mystery. There's definitely times when I should have died and didn't. When a lorry nearly rammed into my car on the motorway. When I was boat-jumping, drunk and I nearly fell on a propeller and a nice chap saved me and said I needed to stop goofing around, God bless him. And when I drove across Spain at night with no lights on and didn't realise until I got to my destination. Could not work out what all the beeping was about!

I'm hoping to get old and die of natural causes, around eight-five should do it. That will be YOUNG by then. I'll be a hip eighty-five-year-old. In that I'll have one hip.

For a long time I didn't tell anyone my age, I didn't lie about it (except on Bumble, Tinder and Hinge), I just avoided it or said I didn't want to divulge it, because the industry I'm in is sexist and ageist. But actually it was me who wasn't comfortable with it and it all starts with us individually. If I'm truly accepting of something, I don't need everyone else to be. Helen Mirren isn't squirming around trying to be something she's not. Arguably, Helen

Mirren has achieved more than me, but if we're holding ourselves up to HM, we'll all be disappointed.

We are trained to think our value in society, if you're a man, is to be powerful (measured by money, social influence, and in a small part fuckability) and for a woman, well, mainly, just fuckability. And youth has become entrenched in that – like you have more to offer if you are fresher, but less experienced. Easier to fuck, and easier to fuck-off. Of course there are lots of men who are ashamed of their age and in denial too. We should all just hang out with each other, learn how to play bridge and embrace our grey hairs and emotional depths.

Some people say they'd like to be younger but with the wisdom of their years, but the whole point of life is balance; there are pros and cons to every age – so let's enjoy them all. We know more than ever right now, so let's not fritter this time away by wishing for something else, like we did when we were young and insecure.

Nature is spectacular though; if we are lucky, we get ravished by time and things start to deteriorate, so you slowly corrode.

It's clever, because, if the people you love have the luxury of getting old, you lose the person piece by piece. You can even get to a point where you want a loved one to go, because they've lost their faculties, or they're in pain. It makes it somewhat easier. The waves of life slowly lapping away at someone, until it's time to take them away on the last tide.

It's the same with our own demise, if we are lucky to slowly dance towards death. We get used to the sagging skin, the weakening of the senses, the increasing fragility, and it makes our grip on the physical world lessen, so that we can let go more peacefully.

The world is increasingly shaped for the young, so as we age and teeter closer to the edge of expiration, we accept it more because we are moving towards a slower life and a stiller place. We shed ourselves, sometimes unwillingly, yes, but there's no denying it makes us a lighter traveller.

I'm going to try and accept ageing – heck, I might even try and enjoy every age. I follow some pretty cool eighty-year-olds on Instagram, Instagran, etc. and they are having a bloody laugh, to be fair. Wearing bright colours, consuming what they want, saying how they feel. There's a freedom in ageing, like on the last night of a holiday in a far-flung destination, you know you're going home tomorrow, so go hell for leather, love. WILD ABANDON. I showed one of these women to my mum, an eighty-year-old in bright PVC, and she said, 'Yes, dear, she's a sex worker.' Well knock me down with her feather boa, hats off to the old girl.

There's also a ninety-two-year-old I saw online who was doing gymnastics, and pretty glorious gymnastics at that. Very inspiring. I've got it all sewn up, I'm preparing for old age by doing yoga (once a month). I'm going to cartwheel to the doors of death and when I get there I'll shout: 'COOOOEY! I MUST BE EARLY!'

Funerals are an excellent ritual, it's nice to have a service and a send-off and let's face it, a sandwich.

A Poem – It's Not What He Would Have Wanted

My uncle (my stepdad's brother) died quite suddenly from throat cancer in his early forties and it was really bloody sad. He was an absolute riot and he left behind a lovely wife and two kids who adored him. I didn't want everyone to be sad but obviously there wasn't a lot I could do. OR WAS THERE? Perhaps I could heal them with my art. I was an average eleven-year-old who never read poetry or books – the ideal candidate to write a poem. I gathered my immediate family in the kitchen to hear my ode to Uncle Richard. I lined them up, picked up my notebook and earnestly read the following poem:

'Death is here death has gone, what's ahead now death has won.'

Yes, no wonder my stepdad didn't take to me. There's always two sides to a story.

They didn't ask me to read it at the funeral, Richard's wife and children had suffered enough. They all sort of looked at the floor and then muttered that they had to get on with things.

I am incredibly, insanely lucky to get to this ripe old age and the closest person to me who has died is my stepdad, who had made it all the way to seventy-five! And I know it was his time (and he loved being on time), and I'm pretty sure he's happier. Of course I can't prove it, but then you can't prove he isn't. And to be honest, he must be happier because the bar was set pretty low in his life. He was very grumpy on this little planet certainly. But then he also had a big bellowing laugh and he was so much fun. No one is one thing. Heaven knows Jimmy Savile did some charity work. Not that I am comparing my stepdad to Jimmy Savile. I want to be abundantly clear about that.

Rituals around death are cathartic – helping us process it and say goodbye. Funerals are an excellent ritual, it's nice to have a service and a send-off and let's face it, a sandwich.

Even animals do rituals. Chimpanzee mothers often carry dead infants in their arms for some time after death. Chimps have also been observed spending time with a deceased member of the tribe after they have died, sometimes tending to the body. Elephants have been seen to mourn other elephant friends after they pass, sometimes covering the body with leaves and sticks. And heaven knows, a ritual for a dead rabbit in a pet shop can be as simple as sacking a child. No, I swear the rabbit was fine.

My friend Jules, you remember her, the one with a big ~~mouth~~ heart? The gal who changed my life! She had a cat who recently died – car accident, if you must know. Don't let your cats drive!! No, it got run over, as is often the way. I'm all for electric cars but they should have a low-level cat deterrent noise built in, perhaps it could bark when going through a village, or play a song from the musical *Cats* – I don't know, have fun with it. The point is my great invention doesn't exist yet, so Jules's cat died and the whole family were bereft. A real lesson to me to get on *Dragon's Den* and stop procrastinating.

And this cat was really good friends with the cat next door and when it died, its best cat mate was depressed for weeks. Isn't that heartbreaking? He missed her and was thoroughly depressed. They gave him her old bed and he slept in it looking sad. Animals are little souls, how can we keep them cooped up in pet shops? They are little souls with feelings and friends and joy and grief!

Anyhow, Jules and her boyfriend and their two little kids were heartbroken. And then a weird thing happened. In losing that cat, the boyfriend realised what was important to him – he realised that life is short, and not to take anything for granted. He decided to ask Jules to marry him.

So he gathered everyone in the garden, Come on kids, Daddy has a big announcement. The kids weren't best pleased as he was cutting into cartoon time, but that could wait, he said – this was big!

He got everyone lined up – as it happened, next to the cat grave – in the drizzling rain. And his speech went something like this:

Him: 'You all mean so much to me and I know I work long hours and I am sometimes grumpy but you are my family and I love you all so much.'

Loulou: (two years old): 'Cartoons now, Daddy.'

Him: 'And I want you all here because (looks at his girlfriend) I love you and I want to know if you will be my wife, will you marry me?'

Loulou: 'No, Daddy, I won't marry you. Stop asking. I just want to watch cartoons.'

So death affects us all in different ways. Some people just won't budge and marry their father, even after a death!

Death is a downer for sure, but even in the darkness there are cracks of light. Though girlies don't go killing your cats on the off-chance he finally pops the question! I know what you gals are like!

I find comedy helps in death, it's such a weird concept, you have to joke. You aren't going to see this one again. Oh OK, I mean it's mad. Like a film but it's real. You have to make jokes to cope I think – well, at least I do. It's a release. I think crying and laughing are similar – in the way that nerves and excitement are. At least with humour you get a laugh as you try and shift the emotion.

Death makes us realise we should say things in life to our loved ones, iron out the issues, get closure on things before the final closure of death. Saying things to a corpse means you left it too late, although it's better than nothing surely? The corpse's ears might just still work, or the soul might be hanging about for a bit to see what people are talking about – I would.

When I was thirteen, I got thinking about my funeral, and got planning just in case. I said to my mum, 'I want everyone to have a single red rose and put it on the coffin, one by one.' And she quite rightly said, 'Louise, you are thirteen, how about you stop thinking about yourself dying? It's very narcissistic.' And I said, 'What's narcissistic?' and she explained: 'Well, the "u" comes before "i" in Louise, babe.'

No, I was narcissistic and I'm grateful she helped me see that. The joke is on her that I get to write that in a book all about... ME!

Just because it's extraordinary, it doesn't mean it can't be real: octopuses and seahorses exist and we are just getting on with our lives, barely mentioning them.

Spiritual Kinks

Look, at the end of the day, I don't even own a kaftan, but I just think there's more to life than what we can see.

I know this spiritual chapter may alienate some people. Alienate has got the word ALIEN in – coincidence?? THEY'RE WATCHING US. I jest. Although other life forces like 'aliens' probably do exist. I mean it's arrogant to think we are the only ones on any planet. We're thick as bricks, if we made it here, surely some of the little green things with *two* heads would have figured it out?

I am aware some of this section is going to sound nuts if you haven't experienced something similar, but doesn't everything? Just because it's extraordinary, it doesn't mean it can't be real: octopuses and seahorses exist and we are just getting on with our lives, barely mentioning them. But just imagine explaining an octopus to someone who'd never seen one, they'd think you were bonkers.

Because energy workers have helped me so much I did go through a bit of an addictive phase where I sort of outsourced my power and happiness to them. Any problem, I would think, Well, I need to give my healer a call. The healer was my dealer!

But my favourite healer (we've all got one) picked up on this and told me not to. Actually, two of them did. The fact I had two at the same time tells you something. And they both said, 'Come on, mate, let's get you to figure some of this shit out on your own.' They turned down my money – that's how you know they're good. The same applies if you date younger partners! The good ones turn down your money.

Of course I've also been ripped off. I went to go and see a woman in LA called something like Cindy Eagle Spirit. She was a white Californian woman and was utter doo-doo. And way more expensive than the good ones. It cost me so much money to have a woman in a headdress waft a feather about. So yes, there's a lot of charlatans. And there's a very dark man who has set up a spiritual centre for boys. God help them.

On a lighter note, I went to a Meetup once (it's an online thing full of different themed nights or events in your area). And it was a meet up to get in touch with Archangel Metatron. I didn't know anything about it but I was free on that Tuesday, and I think in the back of my head I thought it might be a good way to meet men – of course it's 95 per cent women. Actually, sidenote: if I was a single man, I would be signing up to every spiritual self-development class, there are so many fit women there. Having said that, it's probably a taste thing because it is a certain type of woman who goes. It's me! So, yeah, not for everyone.

Anyway, what I learnt at this meet up was that, apparently, all the angels have different frequencies, and the lady leading the class had an affinity with Archangel Metatron. She seemed very nice and sincere and I doubt she was on the make as I worked out she would have made about £60 for three hours. And £20 an hour is not bad, but it doesn't immediately smack of being a con woman. Or, at least not a very good one.

I didn't feel anything specifically, I didn't get the chills or have an awakening, and you are sort of looking around thinking, What are we doing? But it's nice to be in a circle of people all with the intention of accessing some purity. It was a smashing meditation if nothing else.

The best bit though was watching this old man. He must have been about eighty and I just loved that he'd found his way to this bonkers group. And I loved it even more when he asked a question. He raised his hand, leant forward and with the eagerness of a young boy, he asked: 'And can anyone just try to speak to Metatron?' Oh my sweet goolies, that was worth the £6 alone.

◆ ◆ ◆

I'm going to shock you now; even though I went to a Metatron event on a Tuesday night without laughing, these days I am not big into psychics and fortune tellers. I don't think we are supposed to know the future. Which is lucky because most of them *don't* know. I've never been to a good one. And besides, our future is always changing, surely?

I've also had some funny experiences with healers. One told me to put some Rescue Remedy up my foof. I did it. Really stings.

One was good until she saw a ghost and went a bit mad, so it's a dangerous game, kids.

And then I have also had some magical, unexplainable experiences. My most informative one was during a Reiki session years ago, with a very skilled guy called Philip, and we actually became friends afterwards though we've lost touch now. He was very intuitive, which is a nightmare trait in a friend. Imagine a friend knowing what you're thinking the whole time. One day a woman came round who was so breezy and cool – she floated in, in a gorgeous coat with books under her arms on the way to an exercise class. I was in painting clothes with flat hair and Philip picked up instantly that I felt embarrassed about myself next to her. He didn't say that exactly, he just said a little snippet about watching the ego and we both knew why he was saying it.

One June afternoon, I had booked a Reiki session with him – at this stage we were client/therapist. Reiki is an energy healing treatment where hands are placed very lightly on the body. They do not offer happy endings. So Philip was doing some Reiki and I was very relaxed, just lying down thinking about nothing. And then I felt, and there's no easy way to say this, I felt something come into my body and say that they could work with me a lot better if I didn't do drugs.

I had already given up alcohol but I would sometimes do MDMA at a festival, or mushrooms and very rarely cocaine. So I was pondering this agreement in my mind. And then Phillip said, 'I didn't know you had an affinity with Archangel Michael.' I said I didn't. He said, 'Well he's just come into your body.' I was aghast. The feeling, the timing, everything.

I thought to myself, I am never ever doubting this shiz again.

Lots of people will have had their own brush with this sort of thing and then forgotten about it. Several friends have looked into their baby's eyes after they've been born (hard to do it *before* in fairness) and thought,

It's you, I know you. Or often people have pertained to know when family members have died before they were even told.

I did ask one energy worker why MDMA was bad, because it feels like a spiritual awakening and it's quicker, and a lot of the time stronger; you take it and thirty mins later, your heart is open as wide as the Serengeti and you love everyone. But he said the reason that it's not wise to access universal love through drugs is that you have no control and can leave yourself open to the bad stuff too.

I did do MDMA at a festival before I met Mike (the Archangel Michael to you). Philip had said in an earlier Reiki session, if you are doing drugs say a little prayer beforehand to keep you in the light.

I took this advice to Latitude festival. And the first night, we did just that. We all huddled together and I said a prayer to the light, and Helena and Georgie said they felt it – they couldn't believe they could actually feel the energy change after I said this protection prayer. And we all had a lovely night.

The second night, Hels and Georgie weren't partaking, so I did the drugs on my own and then went to find some other friends who were high. I forgot to say the prayer, lost all my other friends and got thrown together with a comedian who was asking me to list people I hated in comedy. What a downer! It was a way, way worse night. OK, it's not the biggest scientific experiment in the land, but it was interesting to me. Am I calling Harvard or are you?

I don't see things as science versus spirituality – there's some fantastic developments on each side. I'm not blindly following spiritual stuff and thinking, science is a bit wack. The issue is everything has to be filtered through humans and so often we are the problem.

I think actually
I have too much
empathy. Is there a
tea blend for that?
I need to micro-
dose my emotions.
I'll add it to my
therapy notes.

Heartbreak Hotel: A Very Blue Middle of 2022

I expected my stepdad to die, I didn't expect my relationship to pop its clogs. Ultimately, my stepdad leaving was more painful, although when someone dies, at least you don't ask yourself, Is it because I'm ugly?

And the third little slice of shit was that my mum had dementia. My brother and I hadn't believed that our mum *really* had dementia, until after her husband died and her decline accelerated and it was all more noticeable.

My stepdad died in June, I split up with my boyfriend in July and I accepted that my mum had dementia in August. Not an ideal triptych.

My stepdad died when I was filming *World's Most Dangerous Roads* in Iceland with Ed Gamble. The crew were very nice and Ed Gamble was, of course, a real solid pal. Shame he can't drive for shit. No, to be fair he was a good driver, but he does inject a lot.[21]

We only had two days left of filming, I didn't want to waste hundreds of thousands of pounds by stopping filming and then potentially coming back, my stepdad hated waste with a passion, and at this stage I was still in shock, so I thought I would just use the adrenaline to get through it. The crew let me have little cry breaks whenever I needed them (a lot) and I made bad jokes to Ed to try and get used to it: 'I've not lost a lot this holiday, only one pair of sunnies and my stepdad.' That kind of thing. Ed laughed along supportively even though he saw the punchline coming.

My stepdad died around 4 a.m. and my poor mumma didn't want to bother people until after 6 a.m., so she just sat up waiting. She was so stoic and thoughtful, comforted by the fact he went peacefully in her arms. She had my brothers there and an army of friends, so she told me not to come back in the middle of filming and that she would need me more later. But she never really leaned on me very much. That's the thing about my mum, in the face of the big things she's a

---

21 ... of insulin.

saint and then she falls apart over an email. I suppose it's all enmeshed.

Death makes space at least and one positive thing to happen from the death (you've gotta look for the positives if only to appease Jules), was that at Christmas, my older brother, my mum and I all went on holiday to Egypt – the three of us – just like the early days. We'd never been away for Christmas before, and we hadn't been together just the three of us since I was four, and it was incredible to be as we were, the original crew. We took my mum on a speed boat and a quad bike on Christmas Day and she was so warm and funny and I realised just how lucky I was. I looked at these clever, fun people from my tribe and I was full of love and gratitude.

To see her embracing life made the dementia prognosis even sadder but there's no grief without love, and I am grateful for the love. There was always more than I remembered. I must remember the love. My mum texts me when I am on TV, she's always pleased to see me, and sometimes she sends little articles of interest; she cuts them out and posts them off to me.

◆ ◆ ◆

My ex and I split up a few days after the funeral.

Here's something I wrote when I was heartbroken, very aware that people need my hot take on this because, well, has anyone ever really experienced heartbreak like me before? It's a poem, of course, because I have learnt nothing from my childhood.

A POEM

My heart feels too big for my body. Too raw for the world, you can't Botox your heart.

My ex said his heart is taking energy from every other part of his body just to stay alive. So just come back then?! Or wait until it's too late and I've moved on (next Monday). God willing.

When I'm heartbroken I think I can sing.

He said he loved me but not himself, but I have enough love for both of us – let me fix everything, I'll come running again, trying to fix what I never had. But, deep down, I know that can't be how the story ends.

We wanted different things, but I would have settled for him. Maybe we wanted the same things in a different order, but I would have lied to keep it alive. But I have to say, I'm delighted with all my wardrobe space.

Timing is important. Love conquers all. They can't both be true, take the mantra you need to get by today, save the others to read on the train. My aunty frames mantras, we can't go that far.

People sometimes feel like they are not enough,

but me, I think I'm too much. That is based on at least sixteen people saying I am too much.

◆ ◆ ◆

It's weird, heartbreak, because you can feel where it is in the body, it's literal. I don't think my heart has come apart into two bits, but it feels like it's held together by a few threads. Though, like any wound, it will heal over again, the two halves inching closer together every day, and eventually it will be fine, it will just have a faint scar. A war story. Something to make me deeper, more empathetic. I think actually I have too much empathy. Is there a tea blend for that? I need to micro-dose my emotions. I'll add it to my therapy notes.

◆ ◆ ◆

The Buddhists say you need to have your heart broken to crack it open. Beautiful. Except they live in a monastery and don't date. I've never seen a Buddhist monk on Hinge.

People say that being in love is addictive because it's as close to God as we get. If 'God' is 'Love' then that makes sense. But don't even get me started on what God is or isn't, because I don't know. My friend thinks God is the sun. I think God is love. Maybe the little sneak is both.

Other people say that when someone's looking at

you through love-tinted glasses, you feel seen and held up as the best version of yourself, you see yourself in all your rosy potential, and that's what's addictive.

My spiritual advisor (relatable?) says my last relationship was so fulfilling because he wholly accepted me for who I was. That's nice because you feel like you are coming home and you don't have to pretend to be anyone else. But then it ends and you think, Oh, he ACCEPTED me for who I was... but he didn't LOVE it enough to override his own core needs. He didn't love me enough to abandon his own dreams and sunbathe in mine. But I know that is exactly how it should be, I know he needed to be free. You can't lose your life to others before it's even begun.

I think love is like money or any half-tangible concept: when you've got it, you love it, when you lack it, you loathe it. But it all starts with you (or should I say your parents).

And when your parents crumble you feel like the rug is being pulled from underneath you and you look around for other people to anchor you to the earth. Someone to belong to.

However, the most helpful thing I've learnt is WE ARE LOVE. It lives inside us. LOVE LIVES INSIDE US RIGHT SLAP BANG IN THE MIDDLE IN OUR HEARTS. We just keep running around trying to get someone else to unlock it.

◆ ◆ ◆

The guy who broke my heart was called Jamie and it's the first time I got dumped in a long-term relationship. Short term, it was often them, but long term, it was always me. So, what, I gotta mend my heart and ego now?!

I knew there was something about him, the first time I saw him. But it's hard to know if I was staring down the barrel of fate or just good looks.

I knew he loved me, so it was so confusing: you rake over it and think maybe if I hadn't made him that rank sandwich, we'd still be together. I don't know if you are capable of making someone a sandwich so bad they finish with you, but that is EXACTLY the sort of thing in my wheelhouse.

He wasn't a shagger or a bad guy, but in the end the age gap broke us up. The sandwich may have contributed. My big tip? Don't add vegan salad cream and mayonnaise to a hummus base.

I knew the age would be an issue, he was sixteen years younger than me – ridiculous. And exactly the sort of thing you'll see me having a go at the guys for. Of course he was too young for me – I met him at the skatepark.

I didn't want the seriousness of life to seep in. Though of course, eventually it does. You talk about the future and you realise you cannot walk the same path and both be happy.

When we split up, a very wise friend told me to send him love and picture him with everything: success, expansion, and love – the love of a new partner. I shut my eyes serenely and then calmly barked: 'Are you fucking mad?' But then I did do it, I imagined him with a new girlfriend more suited to his age and stage of life. I don't know what she looked like, but the love was there and it shifted something in me instantly. In a great, great way. And I wanted that for him. Hard recommend.

People say timing is everything, and now I believe them. I've never been able to love anyone like that, I was ready, finally, and the cold, hard irony was that he wasn't.

When the relationship ended and I had to do Edinburgh with a show about how much I loved this guy, and jokes about my stepdad, who had just passed away, I was so, so sad. I don't think I had ever been sadder in my life, bursting with pain and loss. And reliving the relationship every night on stage. I cried every day. I must have had periods where I was sadder, but I didn't acknowledge it, because I was demented for so long, but this year was particularly grim, because it came just after one of the happiest years of my life. There it is: light and dark dancing in the wind together. You have to experience it all.

It seems silly now that I was so sad about that when people lose children, and wives, and have to just carry on.

Now the pain has gone, I'm grateful for the lessons,

the next guy I will make more time for, and let life take centre stage a bit more. And, crucially, be more present for. It used to drive the last one mad that I was on my phone all the time. And what was I doing? A lot of the time naff all. I'd just learnt to disassociate and he was so fully present at all times it was beautiful to see. And something I am going to be.

After we split up, we went for a meal, held each other and cried. I still felt entwined with him and connected with him for so much longer than I thought. Then I got two kittens and slowly healed. The irony is – there's even more of an age gap between me and the kittens! But that's OK because it's more of a mother-son kinda thing IF YOU MUST KNOW.

Often it's not about that person, it's about what they opened up in you. At one point he texted me and I thought he wanted to get back together and I panicked and my body thought no, no, no. But then when he didn't, I went back to craving him again.

The mind can trick you into thinking you need something you don't. The mind is always on a mission to tell you're lacking something you're not. I met up with him to give his stuff back six months after the split and I looked at him and thought, There's my old friend, and I didn't want him back, or need to hold him. I just thought, What a sweet, great guy but he's not mine. And OF COURSE HE'S TOO YOUNG FOR YOU, YOU MORON,

YOU ARE OVER FORTY AND HE HAS A MULLET. I had been crying for six months over an illusion of a thing. Crying over something that was never really meant for me. He was just on loan.

◆ ◆ ◆

My beast within is quietening. I used to be so obsessive, I'm sure you've caught wind of that by now. If I fancied someone, often I couldn't think about much else and I was in danger of losing myself completely, it got all tied up with them wanting me. I had a demented drive to conquer a person and it would fall through before it started because they would feel this intense energy and that's not nice for anyone. It feels like an old man on the bus boring his eyes into the back of your head. WHAT DO THEY WANT? WHAT ARE THEY CAPABLE OF?

Thankfully I can stop myself now, and I know it's not real. I know that 'obtaining' another cannot fill the hole (not a euphemism). I know it's not about them. They are a prop, a drug, a distraction, but my God, it used to feel like it was about them, and only them. While they were the attention of my focus, it felt like they were the only thing that could make me me again. But the clue is in the sentence, I'm the only one who can do that.

So yeah, I'm a bit more Doctor Cool now, I'm a bit more Professor Chill. I have come on leaps and bounds;

I can talk myself out of texting someone AND following them home.

The good news is that when we are in a pit, we seek the tools to clamber out, and after telling everyone else to, I've finally started therapy myself. I did every other type of healing or therapy besides talking therapy. In writing this book and having therapy for the first time, a lot of anger came up and I realised the reason this break-up was so painful was that he was filling that void, and when it's gone, you are forced to look at that and start to fill it up yourself. You miss the person but you also miss the plaster.

Every romantic relationship has taught me so much and every ending of them, even more.

And having my stepdad detest me initially meant that one of my greatest teachers came in disguise. My stepdad taught me so much. He taught me that people can change when you least expect them to, and often when you no longer need them to. He taught me about the depths of forgiveness and he taught me how to roar with laughter about yourself. We could not have been more different and somehow over the years we transmuted hate and fear into love and laughter. What a lesson, what a guy.

Life is long and we are all just borrowing each other for a bit.

**Dig up the dirge!
Dig it up, dust it
off and slap it on
the wall.**

Writing This Book and Where I am Now

I **hope this book has been in some ways useful or** **a nice escape.** Unless you are a masseuse or one of my family and then I imagine this has been quite a stressful read.

I feel very lucky to have been able to write this book, it's almost as if it's helped me draw a line under my old life. I've documented the first half of my life and now I'm ready to start a new chapter in a new book. Not literally, because this one took ages and I will need to create some more stories first.

I'm still a bit unhinged of course but my addictions have got healthier; roller-skating, writing, taking pictures of dog mess in my area and registering it on an app so that the council can come and clean it up. JUST NORMAL GAL STUFF.

Even my addiction to spiritual treatments has waned. Of course being happy and balanced and peaceful is a lifetime's work, and just as you think you're fine, a big life event will stare you in the eyes and say, 'Really?'

But on we go, marching around the merry-go-round of life, lucky to even be here at all.

I've tried to be very honest in this book, which is obviously fucking embarrassing, but ultimately it's better that way. Dig up the dirge! Dig it up, dust it off and slap it on the wall. We are all human piggies and the truth will set us free. If we are all honest, we realise that we are *all* just trying to get by. Sharing our stories hopefully makes us more empathetic and dissipates the shame.

I hope after reading this you feel better about your ups and downs. And if nothing else you can remind yourself, like that babysitter, 'At least I'm not her.'

Acknowledgements

Thank you to everyone who read the book in the early drafts and gave me encouragement, and where necessary discouragement; it's true, no one needs a whole chapter on spiritual signs. Thank you to John Robins and Sally Freeman for reading the earliest draft and for your wise words and suggestions. Thank you to Luke McQueen, as ever, for letting me bang on about the book and giving me some great notes. Big up to Shannon Kyle for the pond swims, the enriching chats and the encouragement. Enormous gratitude, as always, to Julien Matthews for his patience, support, laughter, wisdom, and not knowing what a weekend is. And to Avalon in general, including Katie McKay, Jack Butler and Mary-Grace Brunker.

And the biggest of all heartfelt thank yous to Susannah Otter who I loved from the first meeting. Thank you for getting it and getting me. Thank you for believing in me and letting me cry in your office when you had so much on yourself. A big bow down to Ellie Carr who has been a great force in helping me understand grammar, the process and timelines as well as everything else. Everyone at Bonnier Books UK has been an absolute blessing and I am exceptionally lucky to work with these literary angels in publishing, marketing, design and the photographer – a bunch of absolute A-grade babes. So thank you to Natalia Cacciatore, Eleanor Stammeijer, Isabel Smith, Emily Rough and all the rest of the team at Bonnier.

Thanks to my mum, dads and brothers, and I hope my family are still speaking to me.